AN ESSAY ON THE ECONOMIC
EFFECTS OF THE REFORMATION

AN

ESSAY

ON THE

ECONOMIC EFFECTS

OF THE

REFORMATION

BY

GEORGE O'BRIEN

[1923]

REPRINTS OF ECONOMIC CLASSICS

AUGUSTUS M. KELLEY · PUBLISHERS

NEW YORK 1970

First Edition 1923

(London: Burns Oates & Washbourne Ltd.,
28 Orchard Street W 1 and *8-10 Paternoster
Row E C 4*, 1923)

Reprinted 1970 by

AUGUSTUS M. KELLEY · PUBLISHERS

New York   New York   10001

By Arrangement With GEORGE O'BRIEN

.   .   .   .

S B N   678 00591 5

L C N   68 56556

.   .   .   .

PRINTED IN THE UNITED STATES OF AMERICA
by SENTRY PRESS, NEW YORK, N. Y. 10019

PREFACE

WHILE this book was going through the press, my attention was drawn to an article, by Mr. R. H. Tawnay, entitled " Religion and Business," which appeared in the October number of the *Hibbert Journal*. I am very pleased to see that Mr. Tawnay agrees with me on many of the matters dealt with in my first chapter—for example, Luther's reactionary attitude towards usury, the support given by Lutheranism to the idea of the absolute state, the effect of the abolition of the old ecclesiastical sanctions for commercial dishonesty, and the result of the replacement of institutional by individualist conceptions of life. It is a matter of satisfaction to find oneself in agreement with a scholar so profound as Mr. Tawnay, and I hope that no reader of this book will neglect to consult his valuable article.

I wish to express my gratitude to the Rev. P. J. Connolly, S.J., and the Rev. T. A. Finlay, S.J., for reading the manuscript, and to Mr. Arthur Cox for helping me in the correction of the proofs.

GEORGE O'BRIEN.

DUBLIN,
  January 27, 1923.

v

CONTENTS

CHAPTER I

THE ECONOMIC EFFECTS OF THE REFORMATION IN GENERAL

CONTENTS

CHAPTER II

PROTESTANTISM AND CAPITALISM

CONTENTS

CHAPTER III

PROTESTANTISM AND SOCIALISM

CHAPTER IV

CONCLUSION

AN ESSAY
ON THE ECONOMIC EFFECTS
OF THE REFORMATION

CHAPTER I

The Economic Effects of the Reformation in General

THE more the study of economic history is pursued, the more clearly emerges the connection between religious and economic ideas. So long as the economist was content to confine his speculations to the needs and activities of a scientifically abstracted economic man, he could afford to neglect all aspects of human life except the acquisitive, and all springs of emotion and action except the avaricious. Such a method of dealing with economics was perfectly legitimate, and led, in fact, to many valuable discoveries and useful results. In every science it is necessary to study the actions of particular forces apart from disturbing factors, and accurate experiment and deduction are frequently impossible, unless a real or imaginary elimination of such disturbing factors can be attained. The danger of the method arises from the failure to remember that the disturbing forces are, in fact, liable to disturb, and from applying the results of such abstract and ideal experiments to real problems without allowing for the restoration of the factors which have been temporarily left out of account. It was because the classical economists committed this error that their teaching fell into such unpopularity, not to say disrepute. Having constructed for purposes of experiment an ideal economic man, wholly composed of self-interest and avarice, and recognizing no measure of value but the pecuniary one, they wrongly concluded that the perfectly correct results at which they had arrived by their experiments on this creature were applicable to real men composed of flesh and blood. They abstracted from the object of their observation all motives of honour, patriotism, and religion, and they forgot to restore these motives when stating the results of their investigations. Naturally, the actions and thoughts of such an abnormal monster would not be influenced by ethical and still less by supernatural considerations; and, equally naturally, the economic science constructed on the observation of a world peopled exclusively by such creatures would not find it necessary to pay any attention to the cultural, moral, or supernatural aspects of life.*

It was this elimination of all but the avaricious motives from economic life which produced the sterility of classical political economy; and the restoration of the forgotten motives of love, duty, and religion into the

---

* Dean Inge puts this well: " There is not much fault to find with the old economists so long as they recognized that their science was an abstract science, which for its own purposes dealt with an unreal abstraction—the economic man. Every science is obliged to isolate one aspect of reality in this way. But when political economy was treated as a philosophy of life it began to be mischievous. A book on ' The Science of the Stomach,' without knowledge of physiology or the working of other organs, would not be of much use. Man has never been a purely acquisitive being: for example, he is also a fighting and a praying being." (*Outspoken Essays*, p. 22.)

study of political economy was the principal aim of the German or historical school. As soon as economics, and in particular economic history, came to be studied from this new standpoint, it became at once apparent how deeply the economic life of man was coloured and influenced by his religious beliefs and surroundings; and the connection between these two great departments of human activity would not be questioned by anybody at the present day.*

The influence of religion on economic life and thought will naturally not always be equally powerful, but will vary with the relative stages of development of religious and economic activity. In an age in which people are generally irreligious, and in which no strong dogmatic institution is universally recognized, the influence of religion in the economic sphere will be less pronounced than in an age when everybody is deeply penetrated with faith, and when all are obedient to a single religious and moral teacher. On the other hand, the economic department of human life will be more or less deeply influenced by religious considerations in proportion to the state of development which has been attained by an independent economic science. A people in possession of an extensive literature and tradition, dealing with the economic side of life from a scientific or rationalist standpoint, will be less subject to the influence of religious thought than one which is accustomed to look for

* " Economic science has grown up in Christian lands, and could not escape the influence of its environment. The relations between religion and economics are well worth discussing, even though they are somewhat obscure." (Cunningham, *Christianity and Economic Science*, p. 1.) " On pourrait presque dire, telle religion, tel système économique." (Batault, *Le Problème Juif*, p. 170, and see Sombart, *The Jews and Modern Capitalism*, chap. xi., *passim*.)

guidance in all its daily problems exclusively to ecclesiastical authority. Consequently, the influence of religion on economics will be far less felt in a community of low religious and high economic development than in a community of high religious and low economic development. Now, it may be said generally that the eighteenth century, which witnessed the birth of an independent science of economics, also witnessed the beginning of a widespread decay of European religious belief. If this be so, it follows from what we have just said that the influence of religion on economics was greater in the centuries preceding than in the centuries following the eighteenth.

But even in the earlier period the influence was not at all times of equal strength. The great development of economics as an independent science, which culminated in the work of Adam Smith, had begun in the previous century, and the breaking down of the unity and authority of Christian dogma had been progressively increasing since the first half of the sixteenth century. The further we go back, therefore, the more marked becomes the influence of the religious on the economic life of Europe, until we reach the Middle Ages, the period at which it exerted its greatest strength. What renders the Middle Ages so important in this respect is that it is the only period in history in which economics was regarded altogether from the standpoint of ethics, and in which ethics was included within the jurisdiction of the universal and infallible religious authority. In the Middle Ages anything approaching economic science in the modern sense was unknown. The great doctor of the thirteenth century, who dealt with every department of Christian life and duty, knew nothing of a science of political economy, either in the sense in which it was understood by the mercantilists, as aiming at increasing the prosperity of the state, or in the sense in which it was understood by the classical economists, as stating the principles upon which people do habitually act in their economic affairs. St. Thomas Aquinas, in so far as he deals with economic life at all, deals with it simply as a branch of general ethics. When it is remembered that the science of ethics was at that time dealt with exclusively by ecclesiastics in the light of revelation as well as in that of natural reason, and that the moral life of the individual was controlled by ecclesiastical legislation enforced by spiritual sanctions, it will be understood how intimate must have been the connection between the religious and the economic life of Europe in the Middle Ages.*

This close connection between the material and the spiritual life of man was productive of very many important consequences. The strict subordination of all commercial and industrial activities to the moral law must necessarily have had the result of maintaining a certain standard of business honour and good faith. Moreover, the insistence on the unbroken unity of man's career before and after death must have powerfully influenced the mediæval conception of economic values. The knowledge that good would be rewarded and evil punished in another world, and that man's earthly existence was but the most fleeting phase of his career, must have operated, on the one hand, to render the poor and unfortunate less discontented with their lot, and, on the other hand, to detach the rich and successful to some extent from avarice both in the acquisition and

* Cunningham, *The Use and Abuse of Money*, p. 153.

in the use of their wealth. The Church's insistence on the superior importance of spiritual riches must have had the effect of subordinating material and pecuniary standards of success and of happiness, and of breeding in the individual a sense of the correct proportion of things. It was never forgotten that worldly wealth was but a means to an end, and that the economic function of society was but a single function, which could not be suffered to occupy too large a share of attention without detriment to other and more vital functions.

While the mediæval conception of life strictly confined economic activity to its correct and proper place, it did not run to the extreme of universal or unreasonable asceticism. The schoolmen fully realized that material wealth, like everything else in the scheme of creation, was good in itself, and might be made the means of virtuous and profitable use. From the very first ages of its existence, the Church had been constantly assailed by and had constantly combated the heresy of Manichæism, which was ever appearing under novel and unexpected forms. One of the commonest aims of these heretical parties was community of goods; and on this subject the Church declared itself again and again in favour of private property. Thomas Aquinas and the other doctors of the Church insisted that private property was justified because it acted as a spur to economic endeavour; and the mediæval Church had as little sympathy with the fanatics who wished to ignore this world in order to fix their eyes exclusively on the next, as it had with those avaricious and worldly people who ignored the next world in order to fix their eyes exclusively on this.

The Church was, therefore, no enemy of material

progress, but, on the contrary, approved and encouraged legitimate business endeavour. The religious orders set the example of arduous and unremitting toil to the laity, and many legitimate associations for economic activity—for example, the guilds—were under direct ecclesiastical patronage. The much misrepresented and misunderstood prohibition of usury contained nothing calculated to discourage or to act as a check on business enterprise, and, indeed, a very great development of capitalist trading grew up in Italy without in any way infringing the strict teaching of the Church on this point. If any refutation were needed of the libel that the mediæval Church acted as a bar to economic progress, it would be supplied by a mere examination of some of the magnificent survivals of the period.*

It would be out of place further to labour this point in an essay which, after all, does not profess to be an economic history of the Middle Ages. The point to which we do wish to direct attention is that the whole fabric of mediæval civilization rested upon a religious basis. The regulation of every activity of secular life was regarded as a matter to be approached from the standpoint of the general Christian ethic, which, in its turn, was regarded as a matter to be pronounced upon by the Church. In this way, the universally accepted ideas of commercial men and of people generally of the time were ideas founded upon a religious basis; and the whole complexion of everyday life was coloured by these ideas, just as the whole complexion of present-day life is coloured by certain ideas of its own. The importance

* The suggestion that the mediæval Church was hostile to business enterprise is ably controverted by Sombart in *The Quintessence of Capitalism*, p. 248.

of such underlying—often imperfectly realized and
subconscious—ideas is excellently explained by Professor Foxwell: " That there are such underlying ideas
of right and wrong, and that the whole tenor of legislation is silently, unconsciously, moulded by these
accepted views as to what is economically and consti-
tutionally fair and just, will not be disputed. Crystal-
lized into catching phrases, we meet with these current
ideas of equity at every turn. One man one vote;
a living wage; a fair's day wage for a fair day's work;
equality of opportunity; *à chacun selon ses œuvres;*
property is a trust; a man may do as he likes with his
own; *caveat emptor; laissez faire*—these and many others
will be familiar to us as effective instruments of economic
and political movement. If they are modified, the legislation of all free countries will reflect the change; until
they are modified, no forcible revolution will leave
more than a superficial and transient effect."*

The maxims given by Professor Foxwell in the passage
quoted are excellent examples of the sort of maxims that
underlie and form the groundwork of thought in the
modern unregulated, competitive age. The mediæval
man possessed quite as many maxims of this kind as
the modern man, but they were essentially different in
outlook. As Professor Foxwell puts it: " It would be
hard to say whether the average man of to-day would
be more astonished at the mediæval ideas of corporate
responsibility and vicarious punishment than the mediæval would be at our anarchical competition and flagrant
usury. But it is certain that each would find the other's
notion of fairness positively scandalous."† If we were

---

* Introduction to English Translation of Menger's *Right to the
Whole Produce of Labour*, p. xiii.   † *Ibid.*

to attempt to discover the essential difference between the two points of view, we should find that the modern point of view rests upon an individualist and rationalist basis, while the mediæval rested upon a solidarist and dogmatic basis. In other words, whereas modern society is fundamentally scientific in its ideas, mediæval society was fundamentally religious. " The mediæval man had an *idée fixe*, religion, which entered as a blend into all his thoughts, political, economic, scientific or artistic."*

It follows that a society penetrated throughout, as mediæval society was, by the ideas and teaching of a dogmatic religion will continue essentially unchanged so long as no change occurs in the religion on which it is based. In order, therefore, to effect any far-reaching social change in such a society, it is necessary to attack the religion in which it is rooted; and conversely, any attack on the religion entails, as a necessary consequence, serious social and economic changes. When in the extreme case the attack on the old religion is directed against its very foundations, and when the old faith is shaken from top to bottom, the social and economic consequences are bound to be correspondingly deep and

* Schapiro, *Social Reform and the Reformation*, p. 98. As Dr. Cunningham puts it: " During the Middle Ages human activities were dominated by religion, while in modern times political and economic life has been secularized. . . . In the old days life had been treated as a whole; all institutions had religious as well as political aspects; but in the course of the centuries the two sides fell apart, and life could be conveniently divided into sections." (*Christianity and Economic Science*, pp. 3 and 76). " In the inner harmony of the system of the Middle Ages the economic order found its parallel in the political order, and was even reflected in the spiritual order, and projected in the conception of another world. The mediæval conditions resulted in a long period of organic and stable society." (Foxwell, *op. cit.*, p. xv.)

revolutionary. The religious movement known as the Reformation was essentially an attack of this kind. It aimed at subverting the basic foundation upon which the prevailing order rested, and at dismembering the whole edifice of existing belief and tradition. Can it be a matter of surprise that such a movement should have been accompanied by social and economic consequences of the gravest kind ? It is the aim of the present essay to give some account of these consequences.*

We are perfectly aware of the difficulty of the task undertaken, and of the very inadequate degree to which that task has been achieved. Our only excuse for the publication of the present essay is the paucity of the existing literature on the subject in the English language. It is not pretended for a moment that the present volume fills, even partially, that lacuna in economic history; all it aims at doing is to suggest lines of study to students interested in the subject, and to supply some bibliographical indications, which, it is hoped, will lead to the subject being dealt with more fully and more competently by some other hand.

It is important that we should make it quite clear that our inquiries will be directed exclusively to the effects of the Reformation on economic thought and theory, and that we shall not attempt to deal with its effects on actual economic life. To give any adequate account of the consequences of the Reformation on the economic and social life of the people of Europe, it would be necessary to write a general economic

---

* On the magnitude of the economic consequences of the Reformation see Villeneuve Bargemont, *Histoire de l'Économie politique*, vol. i., p. 289; Guizot, *Christianity in Relation to Society* (Eng. Trans.), vol. i., p. 229; Stern, *Die Socialisten der Reformationszeit*, pp. 2 and 9.

history of Europe since the middle of the sixteenth century. At the same time, of course, it is impossible to separate these two kindred topics into absolutely watertight compartments, and some reference will necessarily be made to the very important economic and social changes which followed the Reformation; but we shall be scrupulous in confining such references to cases where the actual practical changes had consequences in the realm of economic theory and thought, or where they are necessary as illustrations of the growth and direction of such theory and thought. For example, the dissolution of the monasteries in England and the confiscation of ecclesiastical land was followed by consequences of the gravest character to the condition of the poorer classes; but we shall refer to this very important historical event only in so far as it resulted in the encouragement of an individualistic and irresponsible conception of the functions of property, or in so far as it points to a revolutionary and socialistic spirit, displaying itself in a contempt for vested and prescriptive rights.

This limitation of our subject saves us from the necessity of discussing the highly controversial subject of the comparative progress of Catholic and Protestant countries. While there is probably no one topic in economic history which has provoked so much acrimony and heat as this, there is probably no subject upon which more indefinite, unsatisfactory and inconclusive results have been reached. The reason for this is simply that no agreed basis of comparison exists, and that it is not possible to isolate the part played by religious belief from that played by other factors sufficiently to ensure that some non-religious influence is not being left out of account. The few remarks which we think it advisable to offer in passing on this subject are designed, not to aid either side in the controversy, but to show how impossible it is for any satisfactory conclusion to be reached on the question, and thus to discourage its further discussion by Catholic and Protestant students alike.

In the first place, it must be obvious to anybody who gives the matter a moment's thought, that the civilization of the so-called Protestant countries to-day does not rest on an exclusively Protestant foundation. The history of the culture of the modern European and American peoples extends back further than the time of Luther; and the centuries before the Reformation, as well as those which followed it, played their part in moulding modern character and culture. It is not possible for an observer, standing at the mouth of a great river, to say what part of the water flowing past him came from the source and the higher reaches of the river, and what part came from the lower tributaries; and it is equally impossible for the student of English or German life to-day to decide which elements in that complex stream arose before and which after the sixteenth century. Even so staunch a Protestant as Macaulay was forced to admit that " it is difficult to say whether England owes more to the Roman Catholic religion or to the Reformation."*

Moreover, Protestantism is not a homogeneous and unmixed movement. The Reformation was essentially two-sided: it rejected a large part of Catholic doctrine, but it retained a large part as well. The former was its destructive, and the latter its conservative, side. It is true that the destructive side—the denial of authority and the weakening of the dogmatic foundations of Chris-

* *History of England*, vol. i., p. 44.   (Everyman Edition.)

tianity—proved more permanent, and the conservative side more transient, in Protestantism; but it is difficult to see how this helps the Protestant controversialists in their thesis that Protestant countries are more progressive and successful than Catholic, except in so far as it points to the conclusion that the less religion a country possesses the more fortunate and enviable it will be—a theory to which Protestant historians are quite welcome if they care to adopt it.

The difficulty of arriving at any convincing conclusion in this controversy is increased by the impossibility of isolating religious from non-religious influences. To compare England with Ireland, or Spain with the United States, merely on the basis of their respective religions, is grotesquely unfair; all sorts of other influences—geographical situation, mineral wealth, the fertility of the soil, foreign invasions, internal dissensions, and so on—must also be taken into consideration. If we look at the condition of Europe immediately before the Reformation, we shall see that the countries which have since become the standing example of the stimulating effect of Protestantism were already beginning to lead Europe in the race to industrial prosperity.* Nobody would suggest, we suppose, that the great prosperity which came to Spain as a result of the discovery of gold in South America was due to its Catholicism, and it is equally absurd to suggest that the great prosperity that came to Lancashire in an age when coal and iron deposits were essential to manufacture was due to its Protestantism.

The last example we have given serves to remind us that the standard of prosperity used in this con-

* Villeneuve Bargemont, *op. cit.*, vol. i., p. 312.

troversy is not one that would command universal acceptance. It is the purely materialist standard of increased production, and no account is taken of what is now admittedly more important—namely, just distribution. Even if it be conceded that Protestant countries have succeeded in attaining a greater volume of production than Catholic, it does not follow that they are more prosperous. Indeed, knowing what we know to-day about the evils of large-scale industrialism, it is by no means certain that, in estimating a country's progress, we should not place a highly developed and widespread factory system on the debit rather than the credit side. Even the most extreme Protestant controversialist does not suggest that the problem of distribution has been more successfully solved in Protestant than in Catholic countries; and Blanqui, whose sympathy was entirely on the side of the Reformation, goes so far as to say: " I cannot help acknowledging that, if the former Catholicism did not know how to put itself at the head of the production of wealth, we cannot reproach it with that barrenness of doctrines, in virtue of which distribution takes place in a manner so little equitable in Protestant countries."*

Indeed, it is not at all certain that the colossal scale of productive industry in Protestant countries does not constitute one of the most onerous legacies which the Reformation has bequeathed to civilization; and that the modern craze for more and more production may not be directly connected with the too high value attached to temporal riches by an individualistic and unspiritual form of religion. Another matter, besides the principles upon which distribution is conducted, which must be

* *History of Political Economy*, p. 228.

taken into account in arriving at a true estimate of a country's real economic prosperity and happiness, is the prevalence or absence of charitable works and workers; and it is scarcely open to question that such works and workers abound far more in Catholic than in Protestant countries. But we must not allow ourselves to be drawn further into this discussion, which, after all, is foreign to the main subject of the present essay; we have said enough to show the essential difficulty of the controversy, and to indicate how impossible it is for it to be conducted to any final or satisfactory conclusion.*

To return to our main purpose, when we seek to obtain light on the effects of the Reformation on economic thought, we naturally turn in the first place to the writings of the reformers themselves. But if we expect to find a treasure of economic wisdom or even of economic unwisdom in these writings, we are doomed to disappointment, for precisely the same reason that we would be disappointed if we hoped to find such matters dealt with at length in the writings of the mediæval scholastics. Prior to the middle of the seventeenth century, no separate science of economics was recognized, and in order therefore to find out what writers before that date thought on economic matters it is necessary to hunt for their views amongst what they have written on other—particularly on ethical—subjects. Thus, the

* On this subject the following books may be advantageously consulted: Laveleye, *Protestantism and Catholicism in their Bearing upon the Liberty and Prosperity of Nations* ; Troeltsch, *Die Bedeutung des Protestantismus für die Entwickelung der modernen Welt* ; *Protestantism and Progress* ; Flamérion, *De la Prospérité comparée des Nations catholiques et des Nations protestantes* ; Baudrillart, *L'Église catholique, La Renaissance, Le Protestantisme* ; Weyrich, " Infériorité économique des Nations catholiques " in *Revue Catholique de Louvain*, Mai-Juin, 1899.

great schoolmen treated the relations of buyer and seller, borrower and lender, and so on, as a branch of their general ethical teaching; and, in the same way, the opinions of the reformers on such matters are to be found in their general remarks about ethics, in their practical exhortations and epistles, and in the actual rules and regulations which they proposed for the example of their followers.

It is not our intention to present the reader with a collection of, or even with a selection from, the utterances of the reformers on such matters as would be to-day classed as economic. We do not see that any useful purpose would be served by such a string of quotations, because, as will presently be seen, the actual views of the reformers on these matters, with one important exception, did not differ materially from the views of the scholastic philosophers of the Middle Ages. The importance for economic thought of the teaching of the reformers did not lie so much in their teaching on this or that matter, as in their method of approaching the study of ethical and practical problems in general. Another reason why we refrain from giving such a detailed string of quotations or references is that the opinions of the reformers on economic matters are already collected in some readily accessible modern works, to which the student can refer with advantage if he is desirous of acquiring fuller information on this branch of the subject.*

* The most notable of these collections are Gustav Schmoller's " Zur Geschichte der nationalökonomischen Ansichten in Deutschland während der Reformationsperiode " in the *Zeitschrift für die gesammte Staatswissenschaft*, 1861; Wiskemann's *Darstellung der in Deutschland zur Zeit der Reformation herrschenden nationaölkonomischen Ansichten*, 1861; Erhardt's " Die

On economic matters, Luther was, generally speaking, not merely conservative, but reactionary. He had a natural preference for country over town life, and consequently insisted on the necessity for a healthy agricultural industry, and pointed to the evils which were often attendant upon commercial and urban careers.*

On such matters as usury and fixed prices, Luther harked back to the harsh and unbending standards of the early Middle Ages, and refused to consider the refinements which the later scholastics had introduced in order to facilitate the development of the new movements in commerce and industry that were beginning to appear in the fifteenth century. Indeed, in this, as in many other matters, Luther is guilty of presenting a totally false picture both of the practice and the teaching of the later mediæval Church, which can be accounted for only on the hypothesis of deliberate misrepresentation or on that of crass ignorance. Recent scholarship has pointed to the conclusion that Luther's misleading description of later mediæval society was probably due to deliberate misrepresentation, conceived with the intention of vilifying and besmirching all things Catholic and papal; but that his false account of scholastic teaching was the result of ignorance as much as of

nationalökonomischen Ansichten der Reformatoren " in *Theologische Studien und Kritiken*, 1880-81. Much information will be found on the same subject in Troeltsch, *Die Soziallehren der christlichen Kirchen und Gruppen*; in Ashley, *Economic History*, vol. i.; and in Murray, *Erasmus and Luther*, pp. 238 *et seq.*

* Buckle draws attention to the fact that the agriculturalist is far more inclined to respect the supernatural than the manufacturer, because the latter is dealing with processes all of which are capable of natural explanations. (*History of Civilization*, vol. ii., p. 347; Schmoller, *op. cit.*, p. 476.)

deception.   Unfortunately, Luther's powerfully phrased diatribes on these subjects had the effect of colouring the Protestant view of mediæval history and learning for several centuries; but his gross exaggerations and misstatements are at the present day falling into more and more disrepute in the light of the researches of Janssen, Grisar, Denifle, and other Catholic scholars.   The last two writers have shown conclusively that Luther was grossly ignorant of the later developments of scholasticism.*

Luther's denunciations of usury are violent in the extreme, but they do not rest upon any ethical or juristic basis that we can discover.   They thus resemble far more the moral exhortations of the early fathers of the Church than the closely reasoned expositions of St. Thomas Aquinas.   One result of this difference of treatment was that Luther drew no distinction between justifiable interest and unjustifiable usury; and that his teaching failed to command respect in practice through its very rigidity.   It cannot be too often emphasized at the present day that the mediæval teaching on usury was a complete and consistent code, which at no time went the length of refusing to allow all forms of interest on loans; and that the so-called exceptions to it were not exceptions at all, but logical and necessary corollaries from the ethical and juristic axioms on which it was based.   By reason of this logical and elastic system, the scholastic usury teaching was adapted to every new situation that arose in practice, and avoided the danger of hindering or impeding any of the legitimate or necessary transactions which arose in an age of

* See Grisar, *Luther*, vol. iv., pp. 117-18 (Eng. Trans.); Denifle, *Luther et Luthéranisme*, vol. iii., p. 79.

great commercial development. Luther tore the whole of this beautiful fabric to the ground, and carried back the teaching on usury to the primitive bare prohibition of all gain on loans, with the inevitable result that it could not be lived up to in the facts of modern life, and that it consequently fell into disrepute.*

With one very important exception Calvin's teaching on economic matters was not much more advanced than Luther's. We shall consider the practical consequences of Calvinism on economic thought in detail later, but at present it is sufficient to say that Calvin had a more enlightened conception of the necessities of everyday life than Luther ever possessed. In this respect he resembled Zwingli; and, indeed, both were probably influenced by the relatively advanced industrial condition of Switzerland compared with Germany. " The German and Swiss reformers " according to Wiskemann, " are united in their war against Rome and all the spiritual and temporal evils which the people suffered from the rule of the hierarchy, but the Swiss reformers—at least, Calvin—display a greater insight into economic processes. They commend all kinds of work, justify usury, go further into the distribution of goods, and express a wider opinion on the influence which the

* " Luther was more inclined by nature harshly to indicate the principles he had embraced than to seek how best to limit them in practice." (Grisar, *op. cit.*, vol. vi., p. 90.) He actually went so far as to condemn interest *because* the Pope had allowed it. See Murray, *Luther and Erasmus*, p. 239. On the superior refinement of Melancthon's thought, as well as on his superior knowledge of ancient literature and philosophy, see Wiskemann, *op. cit.*, pp. 64, 68; Erhardt, *op. cit.*, pp. 718 *et seq.* As to how Luther's economic ideas were formed by the actual economic conditions of Germany at the time, see Schmoller, *op. cit., passim*, and Schapiro, *op. cit., passim.*

state should exercise on external affairs than the Germans, who give a preference to agriculture and to simple commerce, who, with regard to interest, only deplore its necessity, and who, moreover, in their recommendations of tithes, which men connected with a system of natural economy, seem to retrogress."* We may leave aside for the moment any consideration of the other matters referred to in this extract, in order to say a word about the most important matter to which it refers—namely, Calvin's justification of usury.

The importance of the revolution effected by Calvin on this matter arises from its being the first serious opposition on theological grounds that had been presented to the canonist doctrine on usury itself, as apart from particular applications of it; and it is not going too far to say that the disappearance of the conception of the unlawfulness of usury from modern Europe may be traced back to the almost simultaneous theological and juristic assaults delivered on the old doctrine by Calvin and Dumoulin respectively.† Calvin explained his view on the matter in a letter to his friend, Oekolampadius, in which, as Böhm-Bawerk says, if he was not compre- hensive, he was at least very decisive. He attacked in turn the authoritative and the rational arguments upon which the scholastic teaching rested; but, like Luther, he does not seem to have appreciated the correct ethical axioms of which the usury prohibition was but one of many inevitable corollaries. Needless to say, Calvin did not go the length of justifying usury in all cases and in every circumstance, but limited the appli-

* *Op. cit.*, p. 87; and see Kampschulte, *Johann Calvin*, vol. i., . 429; Meyer, *Das soziale Naturrecht in der christlichen Kirche,* p. 29-30.

† Böhm-Bawerk, *Capital and Interest*, p. 28.

cation of his new principle to cases where it did not run
counter to fairness or charity. Amongst the exceptional
circumstances in which Calvin says interest should not
be allowed or should be limited were the urgent need of
the borrower, the necessities of the poor, the welfare of
the state, and the exceeding of the maximum rate of
interest allowed by law.* Calvin is thus far removed
from the modern individualistic, unethical conception
of borrowing as a transaction to be regulated solely by
the relative bargaining powers of the lender and the
borrower, and Ashley is probably quite correct in saying
that " Calvin's attitude towards any particular transaction would have been precisely the same as that . . .
of the average contemporary Catholic theologian."†
But Ashley is no less correct in insisting that Calvin's
teaching was, in a very real sense, a turning-point in the
history of European thought, because the justification
of usury itself was far more impressive than the allow-
ance of any number of exceptions. For those who
accepted Calvin as their guide on ethical and religious
matters, the whole method of approach to the subject
was changed, and the whole orientation of the question
was altered. The mediæval usury teaching was, as we
have already insisted, but one application of the general
maxims upon which the Catholic teaching of ethics
rested; and the rejection of an important branch of a
compact, logical, and closely interconnected code involved far-reaching consequences in every other department of the code. What is more important still, it
involved a contempt and disregard for the code itself,

* Böhm-Bawerk, *op. cit.*, pp. 28-29.

† *Economic History*, vol. i., part ii., p. 459.   This is also true
of the English Puritans. (*Property, Its Duties and Rights*, p. 152.)

and for the authority on which it was based; it was the reformers' first great exhibition of private judgment in morality, which was destined to be followed by such momentous consequences. Thus, while Luther and Calvin were poles asunder in their actual attitude towards this particular question, they were in harmony in so far as they flouted and despised the coherent and elastic system of ethics which Europe had enjoyed under the mediæval Church. The teachings on usury of the two great reformers were fundamentally different; but they had one great point of resemblance—namely, that they both lacked any scientific foundation.

The implications therefore involved in Calvin's doctrine on usury were of more importance in the history of economic thought than the doctrine itself. Apart from this one instance, there is nothing in the utterances of the leading reformers on economic matters which calls for comment, as they all substantially accepted the ethical ideals of the Middle Ages, without, however, accepting the authoritative foundation on which those ethical ideals were based, or the sanctions by which they had formerly been translated—to some extent at least—into practical rules of life. No further light can be thrown upon the main subject of this essay by a further inspection of the reformers' writings in search of other references to usury and similar economic topics; and we must next pass on to inquire in what way the economic thought of Europe was indirectly influenced as the result of the teaching of the reformers on other subjects, not directly economic in their bearing.

The Reformation, though entailing colossal social and economic consequences, was not in itself a social or economic, but a religious movement. In this it resembled Christianity, which was primarily—we might say exclusively—a religious movement, but which was so far-reaching in its implications, and entered so deeply into the life of man, that it entailed social and economic consequences of the first magnitude. As we said above, the great fabric of mediæval civilization rested on a religious basis; and it was in virtue of its destruction of that basis that the Reformation possessed its great social and economic importance.*

The Reformation, then, was not primarily a social or economic movement, and its consequences for the social and economic life and thought of Europe were indirect, although they were no less powerful and historically important on that account. We are not concerned in the present essay with the practical results which the Reformation effected in the everyday life of

* " The Reformation was in essence and origin not a social but a religious movement, although, of course, the social and political struggles and aspirations of the time contributed in no small degree to its establishment and progress. Social reorganizations of any importance were only desired by the small Anabaptist groups. . . . The Protestantism of the great confessions was essentially conservative, and scarcely recognized the existence of social problems as such. Even the Christian socialism of Geneva was only charitable and within the existing social framework. Apart from this, Protestantism in the main left things to take their course, after breaking down the forms—for the most part elastic and prudently designed enough—in which the mediæval Church had endeavoured to confine them." (Troeltsch, *Protestantism and Progress*, p. 143; and see *Die Soziallehren*, p. 585.) Max Weber warns us against the error of assuming that the reformers had any economic programme. The economic consequences of their activities were the result—often a result they would have deplored had they foreseen it—of their religious teaching. (" Die protestantische Ethik und der Geist des Kapitalismus " in *Archiv für Sozialwissenschaft und Sozialpolitik*, vol. xx., p. 53; Meyer, *Das soziale Naturrecht in der christlichen Kirche*, p. 26.)

Europe, through its abolition of the monasteries, its disapproval of mendicancy both lay and clerical, its rejection of celibacy, and its secularization of the Church lands. These are matters of the greatest historical interest and importance, but they lie rather outside the scope of our present study; yet we may draw attention in passing to the fact that all these events, of gigantic social consequence, were inspired by religious and not by social motives. What we are rather concerned with is the reaction which the religious teaching of the Reformation caused in the realm of economic thought. It is necessary to emphasize the far-reaching developments of that religious teaching, which profoundly influenced the whole religious thought of modern Europe, even outside the Lutheran and Calvinist communions.

One matter to which we have already referred is the essential unity of the mediæval ecclesiastical system. Whether we approve or disapprove of the Catholicism of the later Middle Ages—that is to say, of the religion of civilized Europe at that time—we must recognize that it was a living organism, closely bound up in all its parts. Its activities were manifold, and radiated in innumerable directions; but, however self-centred and independent they may have appeared, they were, in fact, directed to a common purpose and animated by a common spirit. Any attack on one part of an organism of this kind cannot be localized and isolated, but must, in the nature of things, exercise an influence upon the whole; and that influence will be greater or less, according as the part of the organism attacked is nearer to or further from its heart. " The more consistently a system is carried out," we read in Möhler's great book on Symbolism, " and the more harmoniously it is framed, the more will any modification in its fundamental principle shape all its parts. Whoever, therefore, in its centre assailed Catholicism, whose doctrines are all most intimately intertwined, was forced by degrees to attack many other points also, whose connection with those first combated was in the beginning scarcely imagined."* We need not further labour this point. It is recognized by everybody to-day that the Reformation was an attack on the old Church of such a kind that it was impossible to localize it or limit its influence to the particular targets selected for the first assault. It was an attack that was bound, in its very nature, to endanger the existence of the Church as a whole; and, if we are correct in saying that mediæval civilization rested upon the Church, it was an attack directed against the whole existing order of European society. It was, therefore, in the strict sense of the word, epoch-making from the social standpoint.

It was, of course, the aim of the reformers to injure in every possible way the Catholic Church, which they regarded as the great obstacle in the path towards the introduction of the purer and truer form of Christianity which they preached; but they seemed to forget that, if the Church was a formidable antagonist of the reformed doctrines, it was a no less formidable antagonist of other opinions of which they themselves heartily disapproved, and from which they desired all the protection they could obtain. There is no doubt that the unity of Christendom in the Middle Ages, which would have been impossible without a united visible Church, was of the greatest service in combating the innumerable enemies

* Eng. trans., vol. i., p. 32.

of Christianity who ceaselessly threatened to overwhelm the fabric of European civilization, and also that it aided the organization and secured the success of Christian missionary endeavours. So long as Europe was united in faith, the whole effort of Christian missionaries could be devoted to the conversion of the heathen; but as soon as it became divided, their energies were dissipated in attempts to convert each other. " When breaking the unity of European civilization, Protestantism introduced discord into the bosom of that civilization, and weakened the physical and moral action which it exercised on the rest of the world."*

The Reformation not only weakened the Church in its relation to the non-Christian world, but it also weakened its power to deal with the communist heretics, who had at no time been completely absent from Europe, but who had been severely kept in check so long as the Church was powerful. From its very earliest ages, the Church had always been subject to attacks from sects, more or less infected with Manichæan opinions, which had stood for an Oriental detachment from the world, quite foreign to the balanced and reasonable view of life taken by Catholicism. The doctrines of these heretical sects were quite as distasteful to the reformers as they were to the mediæval scholastics, but the former unconsciously and unwillingly aided them by their attack on the central stronghold of European culture and civilization. It is more than a coincidence merely to be accounted for by a rise of prices or a series of bad harvests that Germany was distracted by the Peasants' War almost immediately after Luther's first assault on the Church. The fact is

* Balmez, *Protestantism and Catholicity compared*, p. 212.

that the communists and antisocial sects gained
heart and courage from the spectacle of an attack
delivered from another quarter on the one institution
that they feared, and that they knew they could not
conquer alone.*

The Reformation not only made easier the progress
of the already existing sects, but it opened the way for
new ones. The main characteristics of the sects in the
old Catholic days had been world-renunciation and
asceticism, while those of the new sects in Protestant
countries were extreme individualism and the unfettered
claim of every Christian to interpret the Bible in his
own way, and to work out his own salvation without the
intervention of any priest or hierarchy.† Of course,
the Protestant churches were in a very much weaker
position to resist the growth of sects than the Catholic
Church had been; the principle of private judgment, on

---

* " The adherents of communistic sects were, in general, too
weak to entertain, in times of peace, the thought that they could
overthrow existing society by their own power, in order to set up
communism in its place. If they were not servile and sub-
missive, like the baser proletariats of declining Rome, they were
still a universally peace-loving folk up to the time of the Reformation, and such evidence as we have unanimously bears out the
fact that love of peace and patience were as much their characteristics as were industry and sobriety. But when insurrec-
tionary times came, when peasants and traders rose around them,
then revolutionary enthusiasm seized the communists also. It
then appeared to them, or at least to a portion of them, for they
were divided over this question, that the time had come when
God would show strength in weakness, and when no miracle
seemed impossible." (Kautsky, *Communism in Central Europe*,
pp. 27-8. See also Morris and Bax, *Socialism, Its Growth and
Outline*, pp. 57-8; Meyer, *Das soziale Naturrecht in der christlichen Kirche*, p. 22.) On the extent to which the Reformation
helped the communist sects, see also Janssen, *History of the
German People*, vol. iv., p. 143; Troeltsch, *Soziallehren*, p. 803.

† Troeltsch, *op. cit.*, pp. 797, 810, 943.

which the Protestant confessions were based, was a two-edged weapon, which could be used, and was used, with deadly effect against its original inventors.   The Anabaptists never tired of quoting certain of Luther's own sayings against their Lutheran adversaries, and the latter were unable to make any satisfactory reply.*   Once the principle of private judgment is made use of to establish one's position, one can scarcely complain if others make use of the same principle to destroy it.   Thus the sects prospered far more vigorously after than before the Reformation, and exercised on the Protestant churches a far greater disintegrating influence than they had ever been able to exercise on the Catholic Church, which by reason of its broader outlook and superior institutions was able to enrol into its service many who would otherwise have been animated by sectarianism.†

* Troeltsch, *op. cit.*, p. 798; examples given in footnote. Nicolas, *Du Protestantisme et de toutes les Hérésies dans leurs Rapports avec le Socialisme*, pp. 192-3.

† Troeltsch, *op. cit.*, pp. 810-11, 939: " It is vain for man to struggle against the nature of things; Protestantism endeavoured without success to limit the rights of private judgment.   It raised its voice against it, and sometimes appeared to attempt its total destruction; but the right of private judgment, which was in its own bosom, remained there, developed itself, and acted there in spite of it.   There was no middle course for Protestantism to adopt; it was compelled either to throw itself into the arms of authority, and thus acknowledge itself in the wrong, or else allow the developing principle to exert as much influence on its various sects as to destroy even the religion of Christ, and debase Christianity to the rank of a school of philosophy. . . .   The only way which Protestantism has of preserving itself is to violate as much as possible of its own fundamental principle." (Balmez, *op. cit.*, pp. 17, 35.)   " The Protestant writers against Rome were forging the weapons which were soon to be used against themselves.   The assumptions which were common to them and to their antagonists naturally escaped any strict scrutiny though it was presently to appear that they were equally assailable by

Indeed, it is obvious that sectarianism is more likely to be a danger in Protestant than in Catholic communities. Not only does the admission of the right of private judgment make it impossible for the Protestant to combat the sectary in argument, but it is the very nature of heresy itself to subdivide. " Heretics," says Tertullian, " vary in their rules; usually in their confession of faith; everyone of them thinks he has a right to change and model what he has received according to his own fancy, as the author of the sect composed it according to his own fancy. Heresy never changes its proper nature in never ceasing to innovate; and the progress of the thing is like to its origin."* The Protestant, Sir Thomas Browne, remarked on this tendency to subdivide in *Religio Medici :* " Even in doctrines heretical there will be super-heresies, and Arians not only divided from

the methods already employed against assumptions actually disputed," (Leslie Stephen, *English Thought in the Eighteenth Century,* vol. i., p. 79.) " Since studies pass into character, it is natural to find a marked effect from this turning loose of a new source of spiritual authority. That thousands were made privately better, wiser, and happier from the reading of the gospels and the Hebrew poetry, that standards of morality were raised, and ethical tastes purified thereby is certain. But the same cause had several effects that were either morally indifferent or positively bad. The one chiefly noticed by contemporaries was the pullulation of new sects. Each man, as Luther complained, interpreted the Holy Book according to his own brain and crazy reason. The old saying that the Bible was the book of heretics came true. It was in vain for the Reformers to insist that none but the ministers—*i.e.,* themselves—had the right to interpret Scripture. It was in vain for the governments to forbid, as the Scotch statute expressed it, ' any to dispute or hold opinion on the Bible '; discordant clamour of would-be expounders arose, some learned, others ignorant, others fantastic, and all pigheaded and intolerant." (Preserved Smith, *The Age of the Reformation,* p. 573.)

* *De Præscrip., c.* 42.

the Church, but also amongst themselves; for heads that are disposed unto schism, and complexionally propense to innovation, are naturally indisposed for a community, nor will ever be confined unto the order of economy of one body, and therefore, when they separate from others, they knit but loosely among themselves; nor contented with a general breach or dichotomy with their Church, do subdivide and mince themselves almost into atoms."* Another Protestant writer remarked on this characteristic of heresy that " divisions among our sectaries originate for the most part in the same sort of temper which gave birth to the sect."† " The want of reverence towards father and mother is transmitted from generation to generation; and the wicked spirit that first raised the son up against his father, goes out of the son as soon as he becomes a parent, and, in turn, goads his offspring on to wreak bloody vengeance upon him."‡ Bossuet says, " That which at the commencement a false light made no hazard is found attended with such inconsistencies as to oblige these reformers every day to reform themselves, so that they cannot tell when their own minds be at rest or their innovations terminated."§

These successive attacks by private judgment gradually diminished the original deposit of definite doctrine which the great Protestant confessions contained at their inception. The Protestantism of the sixteenth century consisted, as we have said, of two distinct elements; on the one hand, the destructive element, which consisted of the principle of private

* P. 10.   (Everyman Edition.)
† Southey's *Colloquies*, vol. ii., p. 62.
‡ Möhler, *op. cit.*, vol. ii., p. 261.   § *Variations*, p. 4.

judgment and the other characteristic doctrines of the reformers, and, on the other hand, the conservative element, which consisted of the Catholic doctrines which were still retained.   The whole history of Protestantism is that of the disappearance of the latter element before the inroads of the former; and it is correct to say that Protestantism has become more Protestant and less Catholic with the passage of time.   Indeed, the continual union of these two elements was in the nature of things impossible, and it was only a matter of time until the conservative element gave way before the destructive element.   It was further inevitable that a point would come in this process of erosion when the conservative element would disappear altogether, or would come to be interpreted in a vague and uncertain way which would rob it of all its importance.   This is what did in fact happen: the ancient Catholic doctrines preserved by the reformers gradually sank more and more into the background; while the negative, sceptical elements played an ever-increasing part; until, finally, all the obstacles on the road to rationalism and naturalism were removed.*

The reformers based their whole position on the infallibility of scripture, and on the infallibility of man's private judgment in interpreting it; but this position was soon departed from under the stress of the very difficulties which were inherent in it.   The fundamental principle of the reformers, that man's unaided judgment was the only sure test of religious truth, which led in the first place to the rejection of the authority of the Church and to the adoption of the scriptures as the only source of revelation, afterwards came to be turned against the

* Nicolas, *op. cit.*, pp. 12, 565.

authority of the scriptures themselves. The assaults of biblical criticism, the difficulty of interpreting the true meaning of the scriptures through translations, and the recognition of certain difficulties and inconsistencies arising from a literal adherence to the sacred text, gradually led to the questioning of the infallibility of the Bible. The mentality which had dispensed with one half of the sources of Christian revelation suffered no great pang in dispensing with the other, and thus the infallibility of the Bible came to occupy a position of less and less importance among Protestants, while the infallibility of their own private judgment remained as secure as ever.* Certain Anabaptists, for example, did not hesitate to declare that the Bible was in its existing form absolutely falsified.† Of course, once the infallibility of the Bible had been rejected, there was nothing to prevent Protestantism from passing into rationalism. Rationalism and Protestantism are both attempts by reason to make for itself its own dogmas of belief; the only difference between them is that, in the one case, reason is exercised inside, and in the other case, outside the Bible.‡

Thus, as the Reformation progressed, more and more new sects developed, each believing less than the one out of which it had sprung, and each accusing the less advanced of being papists. By the end of the seventeenth century, Protestant Europe was divided among innumerable sects, and the common foundations of Christian belief were becoming ever more slender and

* Möhler, *op. cit.*, vol. ii., pp. 152-4; Hasbach, *Die allgemeinen philos. Grundlagen d. v. F. Quesney und A. Smith*, p. 28; Dide, *J. J. Rousseau le Protestantisme et la Révolution française*, p. 12.

† Möhler, *op. cit.*, vol. ii., p. 173.

‡ Nicolas. *op. cit.*, p. 255; Schmoller, *op. cit.*, p. 715.

more tenuous. Finally, all remnants of Christian dogmas disappeared altogether, and the age of private judgment passed into the age of free thought.*

It is not suggested for a moment that all these developments were foreseen, much less desired, by the reformers, but simply that they were the actual, and, it is suggested, the inevitable results of the Reformation. Indeed, as Möhler so well says, " the Protestant rationalists are indebted to Luther only in so far as he acquired for them the right to profess completely the reverse of what he himself and the religious community which he founded maintained."† Luther and the other reformers cannot, however, escape responsibility for what they did by their failure to see where their views led. The doctrine of the supremacy of reason in matters of religion, proclaimed by them, necessarily led to the introduction of rationalism. The doctrine of private judgment is the common parent of all, even the most discordant and opposite heresies.‡ That is why Protestantism is the most radical and mortal of all heresies. Every other heresy denied this or that doctrine of Catholic teaching, but Protestantism united in itself the seeds of every other heresy by denying Catholic teaching itself; and was therefore not so much a heresy in the narrow sense of the word as the parent of a whole family of heresies, a common battle cry and rallying ground for all rebels and freethinkers.§ A French writer in the middle of last century compared Protestantism, after three centuries of disintegration and corruption, to a huge corpse which was still decom-

* Nicolas, *op. cit.*, pp. 152-6. The connecting link between Protestantism and Rationalism is to be found in Bayle, see Nicolas, p. 158; Balmez, *op. cit.*, p. 35.

† *Op. cit.*, Preface.

‡ *Ibid.*, vol. ii., p. 149.   § Nicolas, *op. cit.*, pp. 135, 379.

posing into a thousand new pestilential errors; and suggested that Luther's dying words, " Pestis eram vivus, moriens ero mors tua, Papa !" might be well applied to the child of Luther's creation by the substitution of the word " munde " for " Papa."*

We must not lose sight of the fact that the influence exerted by the Reformation on European life and thought was not confined to Protestant countries alone. The sneers of Morris and Bax† at what they call " modern jesuitical Catholicism " are not wholly without a shadow of foundation.   To say, as these authors say, that modern Catholicism is but the reverse of the shield of which Protestantism is the obverse, is going too far; but it is true in so far as it points to the undoubted historical fact that the power for good of Catholicism as a social and civilizing force was seriously weakened by the Reformation.   So long as the whole Christian world was in unison on matters of faith and doctrine, the whole activity of the Church could be concentrated on the fulfilment of its spiritual and ethical ideals, and the Middle Ages did, in fact, witness the building up of a beautiful and harmonious civilization; but, when its authority had been attacked and its position challenged, the Church was perforce driven to adopt a defensive attitude and, necessarily, to devote to controversy a great part of the energy which it would otherwise have devoted to social progress.‡

* Nicolas, *op. cit.*, pp. 426-7.
† *Socialism, Its Growth and Outline*, p. 95.
‡ Balmez, *op. cit.*, p. 148.   On the defensive attitude of modern Catholicism see Ward's *Life of Newman*, vol. i., p. 365; Conrad Noel, *Socialism and Church History*, p. 204.   Villeneuve Barge-mont draws attention to the fact that among the other sciences retarded by the disruption of Catholic philosophy at the Reforma-

The point we have been seeking to make in the last few pages is that the Reformation was such a deep-seated and far-reaching movement that it would be impossible to confine a study of its consequences to the time of the actual reformers; but that the latter must be held responsible for all the necessary consequences of their action in attacking Catholic unity, whether such consequences were, in fact, foreseen or not; and that they must be likewise held responsible for the reactions caused by their religious teaching in other spheres of life, even though we have no evidence that they ever contemplated such consequences. The Reformation, as we have already stated, was a religious movement in its inception, founded upon religious ideas and animated by religious motives; but it nevertheless had far-reaching effects on every other department of man's life. It is our aim now to inquire which of the religious teachings of the reformers were pregnant with important consequences in the ethical, and therefore in the economic sphere.

There is no doubt that of all the new doctrines taught by the reformers, the most important and characteristic was that of justification by faith alone. It was upon their innovations on the subject of man's regeneration that the reformers claimed for themselves their principal merit. They looked on this as the first and most important of their doctrines, and as that without which their cause could never have attained any success.* According to the Catholic Encyclopædia: " The doctrine of justification by faith alone was considered by Luther

---

tion there must be included the science of political economy. (*Histoire de l'économie politique*, vol. i., p. 312.)

* Möhler, *op. cit.*, vol. i., p. 115.

and his followers as an incontrovertible dogma, as the foundation rock of the Reformation, and as ' an article by which the Church must stand or fall.' Thus, we need not wonder when, later on, we see Lutheran theologians declaring that the *sola fides* doctrine, as the *principium materiale* of Protestantism, deserves to be placed side by side with the doctrine of *sola scriptura* as its *principium formale.*"*

The Catholic Church had at all times taught that faith was necessary for man's justification, and that justification was wrought without any merit on the part of mankind in general or of any man in particular. The difference between the Catholic and reformed teaching on the subject arises when we come to consider under what conditions faith, as the institution of salvation, conduces towards individual salvation. The Catholic Church taught that a mere empty theoretic faith, a mere recognition of the truth of Christianity, was not of itself sufficient to justify, but that what was required was faith understood as a new divine sentiment, regulating the whole of man's life—the faith which was called *fides formata*—that is to say, faith vivified by charity. The justifying faith of the Catholic teaching is positive, not a mere blind confidence. It is true that charity is itself a fruit of faith, but faith justifies only when this fruit has been brought forth. The justifying faith of the reformers, on the other hand, consists merely of the recognition of Christian revelation, and of confidence in the saving merits of Christ. The reformers allow that the possession of this faith will produce charity and good works, but they insist that the latter cannot play any part in the process of justification. As the presence of good works,

* Art. " Justification."

according to Protestant theologians, cannot justify, so neither can their absence prevent justification. Man is thus justified, by this doctrine, even though his faith be completely sterile and inactive.* Calvin departed still further from the Catholic teaching by his assertion of the doctrine of predestination, and by teaching that grace, once acquired, can never be lost.†

It is clear that these new doctrines of justification attacked the body of Catholic dogma at a central and vital point. It is possible that, among the abuses which undoubtedly had crept into the practice of the Church in the later Middle Ages, a too great reliance on works of one kind or another was prevalent among certain individual Catholics, but it cannot be suggested that the Church itself had ever fallen into this error.‡ It is probable that the emphasis laid by Luther on this doctrine was less the result of a reaction against the doctrine of " holiness by works "—with which he never ceased to accuse the Catholic Church—than of his own temperament, which craved for a path to salvation in which moral delinquencies would be reduced to the smallest possible degree of importance.§ But Luther's doctrine of justification was also intimately bound up with his teaching on other subjects, and was a necessary corollary, for example, of his teaching on the fall of man. According to the Lutherans, the hereditary evil incurred by man at the fall, or original sin, consisted in the obliteration of the Divine image from the human heart; and this obliteration prevented any co-operation

* Möhler, *op. cit.*, vol. i., pp. 211-5.   † *Ibid.*, p. 120.
‡ Grisar gives numerous examples of the way in which the true teaching on justification was insisted on up to the very end of the Middle Ages. (*Op. cit.*, vol. iv., p. 435.)
§ Denifle, *op. cit.*, vol. i.. pp. 31 *et seq.*

by man in the work of his own salvation.* The new
doctrine on justification was also bound up with Luther's
conception of the rôle of Christ, Who, according to him,
was exclusively the Redeemer of man, and in no sense
his teacher or guide on moral matters.† If, according
to Luther, Christ was not the teacher of new and exalted
ethical principles, still less was He the model Whom
Christians should strive to imitate, and to manifest in
their lives.‡

Of course, doctrines of this kind could not be confined
to their original limits, especially as the persons teaching
them also insisted upon the universal right of private
judgment. Accordingly, we find grossly exaggerated
doctrines coming into fashion among many of Luther's
followers. The doctrine of good works fell into such
disrepute that some of the chief disciples of Luther said
it was a blasphemy to teach that they were necessary
to salvation. Others went so far as to say that they were
contrary to salvation; all concurred in deciding that they
were not necessary.§ The doctrine which had in it the
seeds of all these developments tended to run into
Antinomianism and other kindred heresies, which
taught that, as good works do not promote salvation, so
neither do evil ones hinder it, and that only the unre-
generate are bound to obey the moral law.‖ Luther
was much perplexed as to how best to deal with his
Antinomian adherents, and in his attempts to refute

* Möhler, *op. cit.*, vol. i., p. 123.
† *Ibid.*, vol. i., p. 249.   ‡ Denifle, vol. iv., p. 53.
§ Bossuet, *Variations*, vol. i., p. 176. On the reasons for which
good works were demanded by Luther and the extent to which
the rigid doctrine was frequently mollified in practice, see Möhler,
op. cit., vol. i., pp. 142, 185, 235-8; Baudrillart, *L'Église*, etc.,
pp. 347-9.
‖ *Catholic Encyclopædia*, art. " Antinomianism."

them involved himself in some dangerous inconsistencies.* The fact, of course, is that these further heresies were the result of the original heresy, which they simply carried a step further. Luther himself had asserted that sin cannot injure the justified;† and even went so far as to say that good works performed in the absence of faith might amount to sin,‡ and that St. Paul had condemned the holy life led by papists, which must be pure hypocrisy.§ As is always the way in heresies, a common root produces the most contradictory and opposite errors; and the later Protestant opinions which grew up as a reaction against the Antinomian tendencies, which had been fostered by the doctrine of justification by faith alone, tended to attach too much importance to good works, and to underestimate the place of faith in the scheme of regeneration.‖

The Lutheran and Calvinist teaching on justification naturally had the result of reducing good works to a lower place than they had occupied in Catholic teaching. Again, by his denial of the distinction between the natural and the supernatural orders, Luther did away with the ancient doctrine on virtue, without setting up anything in its place. Natural morality—that is to say, that system of morality to which man attains by reason of his unaided powers—was regarded by Luther simply as an invention of the pagan Aristotle.¶ The teaching of Calvin went in the same direction. " Catholic theology admits a twofold goodness and righteousness— the one natural, as Aristotle defines it in his *Ethics ;* the other supernatural, inspired by the Holy Ghost. Cal-

---

* Denifle, vol. iv., p. 64.   † Möhler, vol. i., p. 153.
‡ Grisar, vol. v., pp. 46-49.   § Denifle, vol. iv., p. 39.
‖ Möhler, vol. ii., p. 153.   ¶ Grisar, vol. v., pp. 49-50.

vinism throws aside every middle term between justifying faith and corrupt desire. The integrity of Adam's nature once violated, he falls under the dominion of lust, which reigns in him without hindrance, save by the external grace now and again preventing a deeper degradation. But whatever he is or does savours of the Evil One. Accordingly, the system maintained that faith was the first interior grace given, and first of all others, as likewise, that outside the Church no grace is ever bestowed."* It must be obvious that such a view of the inferior importance of the part played by natural morality must have the effect of weakening the whole moral tone of the community in which it prevails. The Catholic teaching promises salvation to the undivided interior life of the regenerated; to the harmonious co-operation of faith and charity, and the concurrence of the religious and ethical principles. Luther, on the other hand, ascribed to morality only an earthly, perishable worth ;† and, when pressed as to what need there was of a moral law at all, seeing that it could not aid in the process of justification, replied: " They who are just observe the law, not because they are thereby justified before God, but for the sake of the civil order, and because they know that such obedience is well-pleasing to God, and a good example and pattern for the improvement of others, in order that they may believe in the Gospel."‡ The inferiority of these motives to those insisted on by Catholic moralists is striking, and must necessarily have striking consequences in practice.

We shall refer in a moment, as briefly as possible, to

---

* *Catholic Encyclopædia*, art. " Calvinism."
† Möhler, *op. cit.*, vol. i., p. 268.   ‡ *Ibid.*, p. 264.

the actual moral decay which was observable among the adherents of the reformed faith. There is no doubt whatever that the teaching on justification was one of the causes which led to this unhappy state of things. " Many well-disposed Lutherans were actuated by good religious motives, and expressed themselves in Christian works. But to the evil-disposed, and those who desired to lead a sinful life, the new doctrine afforded an excuse for neglecting the performance of good works of any kind."* Andreas Hyperius, professor in the University of Marburg, and the best theological authority in Hesse, declared that, in view of the low religious and moral standards of the Protestants, it was necessary for preachers to be more reticent on the article of justification by faith alone.† The connection between Luther's teaching on justification and the growing immorality of the time is excellently put by Denifle. " As soon as the mass of men learnt that the ' gospel ' announced by Luther had nothing in common with the law, which had no other aim but to render us sinners; that, in the Kingdom of Christ, sin existed no more, but only justice; that hell itself should be completely closed; that Christ had made satisfaction not alone on our behalf, but in our place; that, in our place also, He had accomplished the law; that, for our part, we could not accomplish it, so that, on one side, we had nothing more to do than to impute to ourselves the work of Christ by faith alone, by simple confidence; that in the work of salvation all our activity was as nothing; that the only religious act which we owed to God was faith; that good works had no value in God's eyes; that moral activity only related to the secular authority; that there only existed but one

* Grisar, *op. cit.*, vol. iv., p. 466.   † *Ibid.*, pp. 468-9.

sin, that of incredulity; that that of which we had need
was to be exhorted to believe and not to practice virtue
. . .; immediately, all this mass of mankind, at more
than one point already ripe for the fall, were allured;
they heard to their amazement that the Christian
liberty, of which the new preacher spoke, meant the
liberation from all law, the liberation from all duties of
confession, repentance, penance, fasting, and continence
. . .; little by little, they came to look on good works as
injurious for salvation, and they finished by plunging
into the liberty of the flesh."*

In order fully to realize the essential changes which
the Reformation wrought in the attitude of Christians
towards ethical—and hence towards economic—affairs,
we must remember that side by side with the appearance
of the doctrine of justification by faith alone, and partly
in consequence of it, there grew up the new conception
of the Church as an institution concerned exclusively
with the religious life of its members.   The mediæval
Church had claimed to dogmatize on moral as well as
on purely theological matters, and its teaching therefore penetrated into every department of private and
public life.   Anything resembling the modern notion
that religion should be confined to Sundays, and should
not be allowed to interfere with a man's business or
pleasure on the other days of the week, was utterly
foreign to the mediæval mind.   Every activity of man,
on the contrary, was seen to be capable of being regarded
from an ethical standpoint and of being followed by
ethical consequences; and every department of ethics
was conceived as being intimately bound up with man's

* Vol. iv., pp. 48-9; and see Janssen, *History of the German
People,* vol. xv., pp. 472-3.

spiritual life and, therefore, liable to be reviewed and regulated by the supreme spiritual authority. In a very real sense the Christian Church—which, it must be remembered, included the sufferers in Purgatory and the Saints in Heaven as well as the citizens of this world— was regarded as being a city of God; and the whole course of man's existence, which was in no sense understood to finish at death, was conceived of as something which must be directed and guided by the teaching of the Church. It is easily understood how a community so conceived should come to be impressed with a deeply religious stamp.

In a society so conceived there could be no rigid division between the spiritual and temporal authority, between Church and state, such as is common in modern times. While, on the one hand, the Church was political and social as much as religious, the state, on the other hand, was at least as much religious as it was political and social.* " The mediæval Church, with all its extravagances and abuses, had asserted the whole compass of human interests to be the province of religion. The disposition to idealize it in the interests of some contemporary ecclesiastical or social propaganda is properly regarded with suspicion. But though the practice of its offices was often odious, it cannot be denied that the essence of its moral teaching had been the attempt to uphold a rule of right, by which all aspects of human conduct were to be judged, and which was not merely to be preached as an ideal, but to be enforced as a practical obligation upon members of the Christian community. It had claimed, however grossly the claim might be degraded by political intrigues and

* Morris and Bax, *Socialism, Its Growth and Outline*, p. 65.

ambitions, to judge the actions of rulers by a standard superior to political expediency. It had tried to impart some moral significance to the ferocity of the warrior by enlisting him in the service of God. It had even sought, with a self-confidence which was noble, if perhaps over-sanguine, to bring the contracts of business and the transactions of economic life within the scope of a body of Christian casuistry."*

The Reformation changed all this, by the separation of spiritual and temporal, of Christian and secular life. The older Church sought to permeate political and social institutions with the religious spirit, but the trend of Luther's teaching was in the direction of the complete independence of the secular state.† The separation of faith and morality, by which the latter was placed in a position of importance vastly inferior to the former, was, as we have seen, a logical consequence of the new teaching on justification. If fiduciary faith alone suffices for obtaining justification, man's moral faculties are minimized so that charity and good works no longer affect his relations with God. Thus distinct fields of action were assigned to faith and morality, which in the old Catholic days had been recognized as the willing partners and helpers of each other. But, of the two, faith was infinitely the more important from the religious point of view; and the moral law was declared by Luther to have been created merely " for the sake of civil order." This being so, there was nothing more natural than that the maintenance of the moral law should be left to the jurisdiction of the secular state. This dangerous doctrine tended at once to lower the respect

* Tawney, *The Acquisitive Society*, pp. 231-2.
† Grisar, *op. cit.*, vol. v., p. 55.

in which the moral law was held, and to introduce the conception of state absolutism.* Ever since the Reformation the breach between the religious and the social sphere has been widening, until at the present day the average man would scoff at the suggestion that the Church had any claim to interfere in the direction of the political, economic, or social affairs of the nation.†

We must not be taken as suggesting either that the reformers were themselves blind to their moral duties, or that they would have wished to encourage any form of immorality, commercial or otherwise, among their followers. On the contrary, one has only to open the works of any of the reformers or their early followers to be struck by the wealth of moral precept and exhortation which they contain. What we do assert is that the separation of faith and morals and the lower place accorded to the latter, tended to weaken the importance of the ethical side of Christian life, and consequently to lower the respect which Christians were inclined to pay to the ethical precepts of the Church. But there was another very important factor also tending in the same direction—namely, the inability of the Protestant churches to enforce their own ethical principles. The old Church had not only claimed to be the infallible moral guide of its members, but had also claimed the right to enforce its teaching under strong spiritual sanctions; but the Protestant churches, on the con-

---

* *Catholic Encyclopædia*, art. " Justification "; Batault, *op. cit.*, p. 175. On the part played in separating politics and social reform from the domain of ethics by Machiavelli and Sir Thomas More respectively, see Bonar, *Philosophy and Political Economy*, pp. 60, 65, and Preserved Smith, *The Age of the Reformation*, p. 590.

† See a remarkable passage to this effect in Tawney, *op. cit.*, p. 227.

trary, were precluded from both these claims by their teaching on the right of private judgment. In a sense, it is correct to say that all the missionary, preaching activities of the Protestant confessions were a contradiction of the fundamental basis upon which the religion rested. In this matter, as in many others, Protestantism was saved from worse evils by its own inconsistency. The religion which proclaimed the abolition of authority and the right of private judgment did not quite practise its own precepts. The establishment of ministers and preachers of the gospel was an infringement of the individual's right to private judgment, but this inconsistency did not prevent the Protestant communions from indulging in the most widespread preaching. While the ministrations of such preachers were no doubt frequently productive of spiritual benefit to their hearers, their authority and their claim to be attended to must have been very much weakened, not alone by the principle of private judgment, but also by the doctrine of the universal priesthood of man. The Catholic preacher had been the accredited agent of an authority that claimed to be infallible in matters of faith and morals, but the Protestant preacher had no claim to the attention of his audience beyond what he derived from his own education, eloquence, or piety. Moreover, the moral precepts urged by such preachers had none of the compulsory character of the old Catholic ethical code, but were merely invitations to act up to a standard which was approved of by the preacher. The value of such preaching depended entirely on the preacher's capacity to convince his listeners, who were at perfect liberty to reject all that he stated, if it in any way ran counter to their own private judgment, which was in many cases guided to a large degree by their passions and inclinations.*

The old Church was essentially an active ethical force. It was not content merely to preach an ideal code of behaviour to its members, but it strove as far as possible to translate its ideals into action. Of course, we must not lose sight of the fact that it was easier for the mediæval Church to regulate ethical, and particularly economic life, than it would be for any modern church to do so, on account of the comparatively simple nature of mediæval commercial transactions.† But the matter does not end there. The power of the mediæval Church to regulate economic life by moral axioms rested not alone on any mere accidental circumstance of this kind, but on the much surer and deeper foundation that it was in a position to enforce its regulations by direct sanctions. The ecclesiastical courts were important in this connection, but still more important was the power arising from the insistence on auricular confession. The confessor exercised a power over the penitent which was pregnant with the possibility of great benefits, not alone to the latter's individual behaviour, but also to the general social regulation of the community. The avaricious merchant, the fraudulent dealer, or the oppressor of the poor, might succeed in evading the keenest regulations of the civil power, but, sooner or later, he was driven to disclose his wrong-doing to a tribunal which had the power to order restitution under pressure of the most terrible sanctions. It would be difficult to exaggerate the social importance of such an

* Balmez, *op. cit.*, p. 128; Grisar, *op. cit.*, vol. v., p. 65; Flamérion, *op. cit.*, p. 29.
† Cunningham, *Use and Abuse of Money*, p. 153.

institution, or the social loss involved in its disappearance.*

The great importance of the sacrament of penance from the social point of view is that it is one of the most potent, possibly the most potent, weapon with which the individual is kept in conformity with the institution to which he belongs. The whole of history teaches the necessity of institutions. The unguided, unaided, individual action of man can never attain the same harmony and purpose as the action of a society enrolled in a conscious institution; and the gains won by all great human revolutions can only be consolidated by means of corporate effort. To preach the gospel and

* " The best way to feel the inferiority of Protestantism with respect to the knowledge and comprehension of the means proper to extend and to strengthen morality, and to make it present in all the acts of life, is to observe that it has interrupted all communication between the conscience of the faithful and the direction of the priest; it only leaves to the latter a general direction which, owing to its being extended over all at the same time, is exerted with effect over none. If we confine ourselves to the consideration of the abolition of the sacrament of penance among Protestants, we may rest assured that they have thereby given up one of the most legitimate, powerful, and gentle means of rendering human conduct conformable to the principles of sound morality." (Balmez, *op. cit.*, p. 129.) Sombart says: " We must not forget how mighty a weapon the Catholic Church possessed in the confessional. The Lateran Council of 1215 had imposed it as a duty on the faithful to go to confession at least once a year. It is not difficult to perceive how the soul and the will-power could be influenced, and consequently the life of the individual. We must suppose that the business man discussed with his father confessor the principles that governed his economic activities. Do we not know that numerous treatises were written, advising the clergy how to guide their flocks in all that affects life, even to the minutest detail ? Economic activities were naturally also considered, and rules were laid down for their regulation and direction." (*Quintessence of Capitalism*, p. 230. See a note on *St. Francis Xavier and Profiteers,* in *The Month,* April, 1919, p. 290.)

spread the new light was but one half of the duties of the pioneers of Christianity; they had also to create the institution that would preserve the purity of Christian teaching and insist on the observance of Christian morals. The course of modern history has shown, if any demonstration were needed, how absolutely right the mediæval Church was in placing such a high value on its own unity and integrity.*

The Reformation attacked the unity and integrity of the Church, and, in so far as it succeeded in that attack, it undermined the foundations of the only power which was strong enough to keep in check the unbounded avarice and selfishness of man, and thus opened the way to the conception of a society of individuals, all guided simply by their own self-interest, indifferent alike to the welfare of the community and to the dictates of the moral law. " The full results of this change " according to Dr. Cunningham, " did not appear at first, and there is so much evidence of gross corruption in the decadent Church of the fifteenth century, that it seems almost paradoxical to regard the papacy as a moralizing influence in any department of life; but when papal authority was once set aside, there was no power that was strong enough to offer effective opposition to the advances of the commercial spirit, or to suggest suitable correctives. In this, as in other matters, it is necessary to distinguish the aims of the reformers from the changes which occurred in consequence of their action. Luther and Calvin paved the way for a thorough-going individualism both in Church and state, but neither of them set it consciously before him as an ideal."†

* Balmez, *op. cit.*, p. 127; Möhler, *op. cit.*, vol. ii., pp. 21 *et seq.*, 79; Ingram, *History of Political Economy*, p. 245.

† *Christianity and Economic Science*, p. 58.

Wherever the Reformation prevailed, it had the result of annihilating the institutional side of Christianity, and, henceforward, in Protestant countries the faithful were bound together simply by the loosest ties. The ancient moral power of the Church to regulate the transactions of everyday life in accordance with Christian ethical ideals had disappeared; and men were left at liberty to act morally or immorally as they pleased, with no responsibility but that of satisfying their own conscience. From the moment that the reformers proclaimed the right of resistance to authority by establishing private judgment as a dogma, Christian morality remained without support, as there was no longer any authority recognized as entitled to explain and teach it. The ethical code of Christianity, which in the Middle Ages had possessed all the advantages of a system of law, sank to the position of a mere abstract philosophy of conduct. The Church had abrogated its right to be the sole supreme authority in matters of morals, and the only power on earth which remained qualified to issue regulations for the conduct of social life was the secular state. It was this lack of spiritual authority, combined with the contempt aroused for the sacraments and the old forms of worship, that caused the eloquent and sincere moral exhortations of Luther and his followers to fall on deaf ears.*

We do not propose to enter at any length into the actual standard of morality that prevailed among the reformed communities, as this would be somewhat foreign to our main purpose. The subject is relevant, however, in so far as it helps to confirm the view we

* Balmez, *op. cit.,* pp. 127-8; Grisar, *op. cit.*, vol. iv., p. 472; vol. v., pp. 571-2.

have expressed about the necessary moral tendencies of the Reformation. If we are endeavouring to prove that certain religious changes tend to lower the general moral tone of a community and to weaken the respect with which the law is regarded and the sanctions by which it is enforced, it is surely admissible to point to the fact that these moral consequences have actually accompanied such changes. It is purely with this object in view that we refer to the unsatisfactory moral condition of the reformed communities, and we shall confine our reference to the narrowest limit.

If we require evidence that the Reformation in Germany was accompanied by a widespread moral deterioration, we need not go outside the writings of Luther himself, who constantly complains of the moral laxity of his followers, and draws invidious comparisons between their lives and those of the Catholics. In one place he states that: " Our people are seven times more scandalous than others have ever been up to this. We steal, we lie, we deceive, we eat and drink to excess, and we give ourselves to every vice "; and in another place he says: " We Germans are to-day the laughing stock and the disgrace of all peoples; we are regarded as ignominious and obscene swine."* Another of Luther's statements was, that, " We now see the people becoming more infamous, more avaricious, more merciless, more unchaste, and in every way worse than they were under the papacy "; and again, " That we are now so lazy and cold in the performance of good works is due to our no longer regarding them as a means of justification. We teach that we attain to God's grace without any works on our part. Hence it comes that we are so listless in

* Denifle, *op. cit.*, vol. i., p. 37.

doing good."* Melancthon's friend, Camerarius, complained that, " Mankind have now attained the goal of their desires—boundless liberty to think and act exactly as they please. Reason, moderation, law, morality, and duty have all lost their value."† Henry de Kettenbach, an apostate Franciscan, wrote: " There are many people to-day who act as though every sin and every iniquity were permitted; as if there were no Hell, no devil, no God; they are more wicked than they were formerly, and, nevertheless, they pretend to be good evangelists "; and another apostate Franciscan wrote: " The people are becoming twice as wicked as the papists, more wicked than Tyre, than Sidon, and than Sodom itself."‡ A notable decline in the prevailing commercial morality in England was observed after the reign of Edward VI.§ The following extract from a modern English Protestant historian is of interest in this connection: " In the hands of men more logical, or of a less healthy moral fibre, Luther's dogma of justification by faith alone led to conclusions subversive of all morality. However this may be, enemies and friends alike have to admit that the immediate effects of the Reformation were a dissolution of morals, a careless neglect of education and learning, and a general relaxation of the restraints of religion. In passage after passage Luther himself declared that the last state of things was worse than the first; that vice of every kind had increased since the Reformation; that the nobles were more greedy, the burghers more avaricious, the peasants more brutal;

* Grisar, *op. cit.*, vol. iv., 210-12.   † *Ibid.*, p. 209.

‡ Denifle, *op. cit.*, vol. i., p. 44, where many other similar passages are collected.

§ Douglas Campbell, *The Puritan in Holland, England, and America*, vol. i., p. 316.

that Christian charity and liberality had almost ceased to flow."*

The economic importance of the tendency of the Reformation to lower the moral tone of society and to weaken the respect in which morality was held, can only be realized when we remember the essentially ethical nature of economic teaching in the Middle Ages. Protestantism substituted an individualist for a corporate conception of man's economic relation to society, and the idea of Christian solidarity disappeared with the destruction of the old Church. The new view of society was due to many causes, but amongst these possibly the most important was the doctrine of justification by faith alone. The rise of a new generation who believed that a simple act of faith was all that was required for their justification before God necessarily wrought profound changes in the face of a civilization which had to a great extent derived its characteristic colour from the conception of the value of every possible kind of good works, both of mortification and charity. The abolition of the old motives, which impelled the mediæval Christian to undertake every kind of good works, inevitably gave a new orientation to man's place in society. Two particular species of good works, common in the Middle Ages, the abolition of which had important consequences in the economic sphere, were monastic vows and almsgiving.

We do not intend to deal here with the profound

* Berens, *The Digger Movement*, pp. 10-11. Further Protestant authorities as to the deplorable moral effects of the Reformation are quoted in Grisar, *op. cit.*, vol. iv., p. 47; Döllinger, *Die Reformation*, vol. ii., p. 693; Janssen, *op. cit.*, vol. xv., p. 464; Preserved Smith, *The Age of the Reformation*, p. 504; and Stang, *Socialism and Christianity*, p. 102.

influence which the monastic system exerted upon the economic progress of Europe, or the far-reaching economic results of the dissolution of the monasteries at the Reformation, as this is relevant to the history of economic practice rather than of economic thought. The particular aspect of monasticism to which we refer is that of celibacy. This institution had the most valuable results by setting aside a class of persons who could devote their whole lives to religious and social duties, without being hampered by family ties and the necessarily almost avaricious prudence which the care of a family entails; but it had another important consequence in that it demonstrated that the married state was not the sole refuge open to men from the concupiscence of the flesh. Luther believed that certain kinds of temptation were absolutely irresistible, and he therefore never ceased to exhort his followers to make early marriages.* The Lutheran attitude towards marriage had two important consequences: by ceasing to lay stress on the sacramental side of the act it opened the door to the introduction of divorce; and by abolishing the old teaching on the virtue of virginity it led to the improvident multiplication of the population. In a society which has ceased to subscribe to the doctrine of the virtue of celibacy, a wave of malthusian enthusiasm has no remedies at its disposal but those that are worse than the disease. Modern history has shown convincingly the correctness of the old Catholic view that the happiness of a community is not necessarily in proportion to the increase of its population, and it is by no means certain that the rapid growth of a

* Denifle, *op. cit.*, vol. i., p. 16; vol. ii., p. 93; Troeltsch, *Soziallehren*, p. 557.

propertyless proletariat, particularly in non-Catholic countries, cannot to some extent be traced back to the reformers' insistence on the duty of early marriage.*

The second species of good works, the abolition of which by the reformers had important economic consequences, were the great charitable activities of the Catholic Church. Throughout the Middle Ages, poverty, far from being regarded as a disgrace, was regarded as a badge of holiness; and even begging was dignified by the example of the mendicant friars. Europe was thickly covered with institutions for the relief of every variety of poverty and suffering, and the resources of the monastic establishments were supplemented by private alms, the giving of which was imposed as a strict duty on owners of property. The Reformation, by its attack on the ecclesiastical foundations, deprived the poor of the former of these modes of relief, and greatly diminished the latter by its insistence on the doctrine of justification by faith alone.†

Luther and the other reformers endeavoured to stimulate a spirit of charity in their followers, but they did not seem to realize that they had taken away the principal inducement to such good works. Many of

* Grisar, *op. cit.*, vol. vi., pp. 61-2; Balmez, *op. cit.*, pp. 102, 111.

† On the old Catholic charities see Grisar, *op. cit.*, vol. vi., pp. 43-6; Balmez, *op. cit.*, p. 144. Miss Elizabeth Speakman in her essay on the " Rule of Saint Augustine," in Tout and Tait's *Historical Studies*, p. 68, says: " The Middle Age was not humanitarian; it had no shrieking philanthropies, for in its relentless logic the things of the flesh were of no moment; yet it developed a system of sick and poor relief which, in efficiency, has never been equalled, and which, in its union of ideal with practical ministry, puts to shame the modern palliatives of pauperism."

Luther's attempts at organizing voluntary charity among his followers broke down, and he was driven to complain of the want of charity among his disciples, and reluctantly to admit that they had been more charitable under the old faith. His ignorance of the world prevented him from seeing that faith alone, without any law, was incapable of begetting good works and charity.*

It was principally because the old springs of charitable activity were dried up by the Reformation that it is correct to say that Luther was the parent and originator of the modern system of public relief of the poor—a claim which is often put forward by his admirers as one of his greatest claims to admiration.† Certainly, some new system of poor relief was made necessary by the destruction of the old system; but, in order to say whether the maker of this great change deserves congratulation or not upon his achievement, we must inquire whether or not the new system was superior to that which it displaced. Generally speaking, the charity of modern times is administered by the state or by the local authorities, whereas that of the Middle Ages was administered by private individuals or voluntary organizations. While the effect of such relief on the recipient may be the same in both cases, there is no doubt that its effect on the donor was immeasurably superior in the old system. The funds

* Grisar, *op. cit.*, vol. v., pp. 53, 59-60; and see vol. iv., p. 478, where many of Luther's complaints are quoted; *Property, Its Duties and Rights*, pp. 154-5. Preserved Smith in *The Age of the Reformation*, p. 557, says, " Nor was there then much pity for the poor. The charity and worship for ' apostolic poverty ' of the Middle Ages had ceased, nor had that social kindness, so characteristic of our own time that it is affected even by those who do not feel it, arisen."

† Grisar, *op. cit.*, vol. v., pp. 64-5.

needed for modern relief are raised by compulsory taxation, the contributors to which derive no merit from paying them, whereas the mediæval system was productive of great grace and merit to the almsgivers.* Moreover, it is highly probable that, great though the extent of poor relief is to-day in all civilized countries, it would have been much greater and more effective if the Catholic Church had been permitted to retain her dominion over European life. Had it not been for the Reformation there would almost certainly have been produced in the Church some general system of charity, which, organized on a grand scale, and in conformity with the new progress of society, would have been able to prevent, or at least effectually to remedy, the disgrace of pauperism, which is one of the greatest evils of modern Europe. And it is by no means certain that one of the results of the change from the ancient to the modern system of charitable relief has not been to encourage the growth of an idle pauper class, living on the rates, and greatly increasing the cost of poor law administration. " Who knows," asks Blanqui, a writer of strong Protestant sympathy, " whether the poor tax has not contributed to multiply the poor more in England than in Spain, by securing to them, at the expense of the parishes, a regular and compulsory revenue ?"†

But possibly the most regrettable result of the change from the mediæval to the modern system of poor relief is that it has rendered the receipt of relief despicable, and that poverty has come in modern times to be looked on as a disgrace. The desire of the reformers to put an

* Balmez, *op. cit.*, p. 145; Baudrillart, *Études de Philosophie Morale*, vol. ii., pp. 426-7; Champagny, *La Bible et l'Économie politique*, pp. 43 *sq.*

† *History of Political Economy*, p. 223.

end to mendicancy, and to ensure that, as far as possible, the Biblical injunction that none should eat but those who worked should be applied literally, led them to impute a certain degree of moral disapprobation to the receipt of alms except by the sick and disabled, and the poor laws of the reformed countries tended to take on a degree of harshness towards the poor, which was happily absent in Catholic days.* It is only too true that in modern times, in spite of the proverb to the contrary, poverty is considered a disgrace. " In vain," says Blanqui, " did Protestantism produce, in contrast to the blind charity of the Catholics, the severity of the poor laws; there has been only one result from them, which is that the poor of Protestant countries are obliged to hide their poverty, while those of Catholic countries can exhibit it without fear; but the wretchedness is not the less real in the two camps."† The modern Protestant feeling towards poverty is analogous to that displayed by the Jews in the Old Testament, where wealth was regarded as the tangible proof of God's favour, as the recompense of the good man, and poverty as a punishment.‡

In view of the extent to which the new conception of poor relief operated to weaken the dignity and the resources of the poor, it is not surprising that certain modern historians have come to regard the Reformation as the turning-point in the history of the European poor, when they were finally condemned to the abysses of despair which we see everywhere to-day. Döllinger

* Troeltsch, *Soziallehren*, p. 576; Cunningham, *Christianity and Economic Science*, p. 67.

† *Op. cit.*, p. 223.

‡ Batault, *op. cit.*, p. 171. On the contempt felt for poverty in modern England see Flamérion, *op. cit.*, pp. 52-3.

says that, " The depression, detriment, and spoliation of the lower classes have everywhere followed on the revolutionary change called the Reformation."* The following is a remarkable admission from the pen of a Protestant: " The Reformation, as it is called, was engendered in lust, brought forth in hypocrisy and perfidy, and cherished and fed by devastation, plunder, and by rivers of innocent blood; and, as to its more remote consequences, they are some of them now before us in that misery, that beggary, that nakedness, that hunger, that everlasting wrangling and spite, which now stare us in the face, and stun our ears at every turn, and which the Reformation has given us in exchange for the ease and happiness and harmony and Christian charity enjoyed so abundantly and for so many ages by our Catholic forefathers."†

The Reformation was an essentially revolutionary movement which cut at the base of the existing religion of Europe, and consequently at the political and social

* *The Church and the Churches*, p. 148.

† Cobbett, *History of the Reformation*, p. 3. On the terribly impoverishing effects of the English Reformation in particular see Gasquet, *Henry VIII. and the English Monasteries*, pp. 460 *et seq.;* Campbell, *The Puritan in Holland, England, and America*, vol. i., p. 312; Beer, *History of British Socialism*, vol. i., p. 44; Gairdner's article on Henry VIII. in *The Cambridge Modern History*, vol. ii., p. 467; Conrad Noel, *Socialism and Church History*, pp. 210, 214-6; Southey, *Sir Thomas More*, vol. i., p. 88; Gasquet's conclusion is: " The momentous social results of sweeping away the monastic houses may be summed up in a few words. The creation of a large class of poor to whose poverty was attached the stigma of crime; the division of class from class, the rich mounting up to place and power, the poor sinking to lower depths; destruction of custom as a check upon the exactions of landlords; the loss by the poor of their foundations of schools and universities; and the passing away of ecclesiastical riches into the hands of lay owners." (*Henry VIII. and the English Monasteries*, pp. 476-7.)

life as well, as the latter was founded upon and rooted in the former. We cannot sufficiently emphasize this point, which seems in danger of being forgotten in modern times. In the Middle Ages civil society rested on the Church, and the Church upon faith; and an attack therefore upon faith or religion in the Middle Ages was something different from, and much more serious than, a similar attack to-day, because it meant an attack on civil society itself. The Church in the Middle Ages was just as much the protector of all ordered society as the state is to-day, and heresy was therefore regarded with the same disfavour that is extended to anarchism to-day. It was felt—as is felt in the case of anarchism—that it was no ordinary offence, because, far from being merely a breach of the law, it was a challenge to the very authority of the law itself, and was thus a profoundly antisocial crime.* " Not only do all the religions in history " says Brunetière, " appear to us as being ' sociologies '—and that is what Catholicism means to say when it says that the Church is a complete society—but, moreover, one cannot lay hands on the integrity of a religion by purely religious motives, without social consequences resulting; every heresy contains the germ of a revolution."† If this be true of all religions, how much more true is it of the Catholicism of the Middle Ages !

What gave the Reformation its peculiarly revolutionary character was that it insisted on the right of everybody to criticize by the light of his private judgment a system which rested essentially on authority. Once the infallibility of the great religious teaching body

* Nicolas, *op. cit.*, pp. 81-2.
† *Sur les Chemins de la Croyance;* quoted in Vandervelde, *Essais Socialistes,* p. 120.

that dominated the world was questioned, no social or political institution could escape jealous scrutiny. " It will be admitted by all unbiassed judges," says Buckle, " that the Protestant Reformation was neither more nor less than an open rebellion. Indeed, the mere mention of private judgment, on which it was avowedly based, is enough to substantiate this fact. To establish the right of private judgment was to appeal from the Church to individuals; it was to increase the play of each man's intellect; it was to test the opinions of the priesthood by the opinions of laymen; it was, in fact, a rising of the scholars against their teachers; of the ruled against the rulers."*

The reforming spirit, when carried from religion into politics, led to the questioning of all temporal authority and to open rebellion. The common people, who were told that they were all equal as priests, wanted to know why they were not also equal as kings—" Who hath made us kings and priests ?" they asked.† " The Reformation "—again to quote Buckle—" being an uprising of the human mind, was essentially a rebellious movement, and thus increasing the insubordination of man, sowed in the sixteenth century the seeds of those great political revolutions which, in the seventeenth century, broke out in nearly every part of Europe. That same right of private judgment which the early reformers had loudly proclaimed was pushed to an extent fatal to those who opened it. This it was which, carried into politics, overturned the government and,

---

* *History of Civilization*, vol. ii., p. 587.

† *Cambridge Modern History*, vol. iii., p. 739. The principle of private judgment made for liberty, and the principle of the universal priesthood made for equality. Gooch, *English Democratic Ideas in the Seventeenth Century*, p. 9.

carried into religion, upset the Church. For rebellion and heresy are but different forms of the same disregard for tradition, the same bold and independent spirit."* The French Revolution exactly corresponded in politics to the Reformation in religion; both were uprisings against authority, and both attempted to place society upon the basis of rights rather than upon that of duties, on which it had previously reposed. Rousseau was the Luther of the political revolution.† Professor Pollard says that " It is scarcely an exaggeration to say that the German peasants of 1525 anticipated most of the French ideas of 1789."‡

The mention of the Peasants' War reminds us that the revolutionary shock of the Reformation extended to the social as well as the political sphere. " The assertion," says Professor Pollard in the work from which we have just quoted, " that there was no connection between the Reformation and the Peasants' Revolt is as far from the truth as the statement that the one produced the other. The frequent association of religious and social movements excludes the theory of mere coincidence. Wat Tyler trod on the heels of Wyclif, and Ziska on those of Hus; Kett appeared at the dawn of English Puritanism, and the Levellers at its zenith. When one house is blown up its neighbour is sure to be shaken, especially if both stand on the same foundation; and all government, whether civil or ecclesiastical, rests ultimately on the same basis. . . .   When habit is broken, reason and passion are called into play, and it would be hard to say which is more fatal to human institutions. The

* *Op. cit.*, vol. ii., pp. 585, 589.
† Nicolas, *op. cit.*, pp. 192, 206.
‡ *Cambridge Modern History*, vol. ii., p. 184.

Reformation had, by an appeal to reason and passion, destroyed the habit of unreasoning obedience to the papacy, and less venerable institutions inevitably felt the shock."* All social and economic inequality calls for an explanation, and a thoroughly satisfactory and reasonable explanation had been supplied by the Catholic Church in the Middle Ages; but as soon as the authority of that Church was attacked, and its explanation of the scheme of human life rejected, the subjection of man to man rested on no other basis than that of force.†

The reformers destroyed the Church as the supreme guide in moral and social affairs, and substituted in its place the scriptures as interpreted by the individual whim of each reader; and they could scarcely complain if some of their followers found in the scriptures revolutionary and equalitarian opinions. Kautsky says: " As soon as the populace in general could read the Bible for themselves, they did not draw from the New Testament the lessons of humility and self-denial, but those of hatred to the rich. The favourite portion of the New Testament to the heretics of the lower classes was the Apocalypse—that revolutionary and blood-curdling imagination of an early Christian brain, in which the Apostle exultingly predicts the downfall of existing society, amidst deeds of horror, compared with which everything hitherto exhibited by acts and threats by the most debased anarchism appears mild. In addition to the Apocalypse, they zealously studied the Old Testament, which is full of examples of peasant democracy, and teaches not only hatred of tyrants, but also active and restless opposition to them as well as to the rich

* P. 175.   † Nicolas, *op. cit.*, p. 139.

and powerful."* " The peasants " says Professor
Pollard, " had eagerly applied to their lords the biblical
anathemas against the rich, and interpreted the beati-
tudes as a promise of redress for the wrongs of the
poor. . . . They did not regard poverty as compatible
with the ' divine justice ' to which they appealed;"†
and Dr. R. H. Murray tells us that, " like heady wine,
the reading of the Bible intoxicated and exalted them,
leading not to revolution, but to absolute anarchy."‡
We must recollect that social revolution was considered
in the light of a religious duty by many of the early
Protestants, who were consumed by the rage for des-
troying all the monuments and symbols of the old faith;§
while, at the same time, the disruption of political order,
caused by the strife between Catholic and Protestant
authorities, made easier the task of the social disturbers.‖

The question will be asked why, in the presence of
such a devastating and revolutionary influence, the
whole of European society did not collapse. The answer
to this question is that Protestantism was saved by its
very inconsistency. Having founded itself upon the
principle of unlimited private judgment, it refused to
allow others to apply the same principle. The very
basis of the Reformation was the rejection of all authority,
and the liberty of the individual to mould his own

* *Communism in Central Europe*, p. 27.

† *Cambridge Modern History*, vol. ii., p. 192.

‡ *Erasmus and Luther*, p. 241; and see Schapiro, *op. cit.*,
pp. 29, 74.

§ Janssen, *op. cit.*, vol. iv., p. 206.

‖ Pollard in *Cambridge Modern History*, vol. ii., p. 222. The
necessary revolutionary consequences of a religious reformation
were clearly foreseen and warned against by Erasmus. (Gasquet,
England under the Old Religion, p. 9.)

destiny without the intervention of any organization; but the reformed churches themselves claimed very considerable authority over their members, and came, in course of time, to be very important organizations. The early Protestants were quite as intolerant of heresy as the Catholics had been, only they seemed to forget that the denial of the right to be a heretic if one wished was fatal to their own claim to exist. Luther regarded the Anabaptists in precisely the same way as he had himself been regarded by the Pope; and every subsequent development of Protestantism was severely intolerant of those of its members who wished to push heresy one step further.

Of course, these attempts to prevent the natural consequences of the very principles upon which the Reformation rested were doomed to ultimate failure, as it is the irresistible tendency of heresy to subdivide and disintegrate; but they had the effect of preserving, however inconsistently, the principle that some authority must be looked to in matters of religion, and therefore of preventing the immediate dissolution of European society, which the Reformation would have produced, had it been pushed to its logical conclusion. As we said above, the Reformation possessed two elements: the one conservative, being the part of the Catholic body of Christian doctrine which it retained, and the other destructive, being the part which it rejected. So long as any part of the conservative element remained, the worst consequences of the movement could not achieve their full triumph, but, as we already saw, this element tended to grow less and less with the passage of time, and finally disappeared. The working out of the consequences of the Reformation was therefore not sudden, but gradual; and this applies to the social and economic consequences as well as to the religious—or, as it would be more correct to say, the former followed in the footsteps of the latter.

Just as the social and economic conceptions of mediæval Europe were the reflection of the universal acceptance of the Catholic Church, so the social and economic conceptions of modern Europe are the reflection of its rejection. The mediæval conception of economic life was that it was essentially a matter to be regulated by ethical rules, and that ethical rules, for their part, were within the province of the teaching authority of the Church. Both these great axioms, which would have passed unchallenged in the Middle Ages, gradually weakened and disappeared wherever the influence of the Reformation was dominant; and totally new ideas of the nature of economic and social science sprang into existence. It is not surprising, in view of the fact that these new ideas were the outcome of a philosophy that denied all authority, that these new ideas were frequently widely divergent from each other; and that they were as hostile to each other as to the common enemy based on authority. Indeed, it would rather be surprising if this were not so, as it is the irresistible tendency of private judgment to travel in different, and often in opposite, directions. The truth of this observation is strikingly confirmed by an examination of the two dominant ideas of modern economic science—capitalism and socialism. These are the two great characteristic schools of modern economic thought; they hate one another like poison, and are engaged in deadly battle for the dominion of the world; they **are** fundamentally opposed in their most vital premises and conclusions. Nevertheless, they have a common origin, and can be traced back to a common source. It is the object of the following part of this essay to prove that both capitalism and socialism alike can be shown to have had their common origin in the Protestant Reformation.

CHAPTER II

Protestantism and Capitalism

WHEN we say that the modern industrial world is capitalist, it is necessary for us to define precisely what we mean; and we must begin by indicating certain things that we do not mean. In the first place, a society cannot be said to be " capitalist " simply because it employs capital in the carrying-on of its industries, as capital is necessary for the carrying-on of industry in all stages of society. The cave-dweller who used an axe with which to kill his prey was a capitalist, as also was the peasant of the Middle Ages who used a spade to dig his plot. The conception of capital is necessarily associated with every kind of industrial operation, and the difference between the axe of the cave-dweller or the spade of the peasant and the gigantic factory plants of to-day is one of degree rather than of kind. It is quite true that the volume of the capital sunk in industry is vastly greater to-day than in any previous age, but it is not this that makes the present day pre-eminently the capitalistic age. The volume of capital has simply increased side by side with the volume of population and the advance in mechanical invention.

It may be suggested that what really distinguishes the present age, which we call capitalistic, from other ages—for example, the Middle Ages, which were admittedly not capitalistic—is that nowadays the capital employed in industry is not owned by the workers, and that the profits which that capital earns (to use a loose but comprehensible expression) accrue for the benefit of persons not actually working in the industry.   In other words, the present day is distinguished by the existence of an owning class, who enjoy unearned incomes.   It is true that such a class exists at the present day, but it is untrue to suggest that a corresponding class did not exist in the Middle Ages.   The owner of reclaimed and improved land with farm buildings and fences, which he let to a tenant, and the owner of a ship which went abroad on a trading mission under the charge of a paid captain, were quite as much the recipients of unearned income as is the shareholder in a limited liability company at the present day.   In the cases we have suggested, moreover, the profit earned by the capital employed—in the one case by the farm, and in the other by the ship—accrued for the benefit of persons not actually engaged in working in the industry.   Both these transactions, it must be remembered, were of unquestionable legality by Canon Law, which raised no objections to unearned incomes provided they were not usurious.   So that the existence of an employing class, and the enjoyment of the profit earned by capital by persons not engaged in working it themselves, is not the point of difference which distinguishes the capitalist from the pre-capitalist era.   The fact that there are more persons of this class at the present day than there were in the Middle Ages is simply a consequence of there being more capital.

Another suggestion that is sometimes made is that the modern world is capitalistic because of the abolition of the laws against usury.   But this shows an utter misconception of the real meaning of the mediæval usury prohibition, which aimed simply at preventing the repayment of more than the sum lent in cases where the lender did not run any risk of losing his principal. The usury code never forbade any transaction analogous to what we call nowadays investing money in business. So long as the person advancing the money was prepared to share in the risks of the enterprise on which it was employed, he was perfectly entitled to share in any profits in which the enterprise might result. The following summary by Sombart of the attitude of the mediæval Church towards commercial loans is absolutely correct: " What was the attitude of the Church authorities to interest and profit ? Payment for simple lending they forbade, but a share of the surplus which capital created they allowed in all cases, whether it flowed from commerce or from the work of a middle-man, or from transport, insurance, or from a joint stock, or in any other way. Only one condition was postulated: the capitalist must himself participate in the undertaking. If he remains in the background or if he will not adventure his money, if he lacks the spirit of enterprise, let him have no profit. It is clear from this that before a man might receive interest he had to be prepared to bear the losses as well as to provide the initial capital."* Indeed, it is difficult to see in what way Sombart exaggerates in his conclusion that " the prohibition of usury, expressed in modern terms, denoted: ' Don't prevent money from becoming capital.' "† Indeed, when properly understood, the usury law has very little bearing on the modern controversy about capitalism, as it dealt with a narrowly limited class of transactions

* *Quintessence of Capitalism*, p. 248.

† *Ibid.*, p. 247; and see Boissonnade, *Travail en Europe chré-tienne au Moyen Age*, pp. 206, 373.

which are practically never found in the industrial world of to-day. As Böhm - Bawerk very properly points out,* the abolition of the old ecclesiastical usury prohibition merely went the length of justifying loan interest; and the justification of natural interest did not even arise for consideration, because its legitimacy had never been questioned even by the most rigorous scholastics. The problems arising out of usurious loans in the Middle Ages were of a fundamentally different nature from those arising out of the employment of capital in industry to-day; while most of the transactions condemned by the scholastics would be universally admitted as justifiable to-day, many of the most loudly denounced features of modern industry would have appeared perfectly justifiable to the mediæval mind. The attack on usury and the modern attack on unearned incomes have nothing in common, so that the abolition of the usury prohibition is not the distinguishing feature which marks off the capitalist from the precapitalist era of industry.

Nor is avarice the distinguishing trait of a capitalist society. As Max Weber points out,† some of the most avaricious people are precisely those who are not possessed of the distinctive capitalist virtues or vices. He gives as examples Chinese mandarins, old Roman aristocrats, and backward old-fashioned farmers of to-day. All these classes are possessed by an avaricious spirit, but none of them could be at all described as capitalist in their outlook. As Weber further points out, there is a certain class of persons—for example, hackney car-

* *Capital and Interest*, p. 59.

† *Archiv für Sozialwissenschaft und Sozialpolitik*, vol. xx., pp. 19-20.

drivers—whose very excess of unscrupulous avarice is really a characteristic of old-fashioned pre-capitalist conceptions. The fact is that avarice is a vice as old as mankind, and that it is as common in pre-capitalist as in capitalist times. The very emphasis of condemnation which the mediæval scholastics accord to this vice shows how common it must have been in that admittedly pre-capitalist period.

Finally, a society cannot be designated capitalistic merely on account of the prevalence of large-scale as distinguished from small-scale industry. There were many quite extensive manufactures carried on in the Italian cities in the sixteenth century, but nobody would suggest that the industrial society of that time bore a capitalist stamp; while, as Max Weber points out, the distinctive modern point of view which we recognize as capitalist was to be found in the northern states of the American Union before any large-scale industries had been introduced into America.* The phenomenon which we designate capitalism is present only when industry founded upon a capitalist basis is conducted by a community animated by a distinctive point of view.† What is this point of view, and whence its origin ?

Probably the most characteristic feature of this new point of view, which we may call the capitalistic spirit, is that the accumulation of wealth is looked on as a good in itself. In the case of the producer in the pre-capitalist era, enjoyment or consumption of some

---

* *Archiv*, vol. xx., p. 18, and vol. xxx., p. 200.   As Troeltsch reminds us, the capitalist spirit " did not arise with the banking business of the late Middle Ages, with the capitalism of the Renaissance, or the Spanish colonization." (*Protestantism and Progress*, p. 134.)

† Troeltsch, *Soziallehren*, pp. 714-6.

kind was regarded as the ultimate end of all economic effort; but, in the case of the person animated by the capitalist spirit, accumulation is regarded as a motive to be pursued for its own sake. This leads to an insatiable appetite for the saving of more and more wealth, which, being in its turn employed for productive purposes, tends still further to accumulate.* In other words, business for business' sake has become the watchword of the modern capitalist. His wealth is not designed for himself or for his own enjoyment; it has ceased to be a means and has become an end; and success in business is not regarded as desirable because of the opportunities of leisure and of enjoyment which it provides, but because it is the outward and visible sign of the successful accomplishment of a vocation. The glorification of business success has resulted in a simplification of the aims and purposes of life; prosperity being regarded as an end in itself has introduced a quantitative standard by which man's fulfilment of his purpose may be measured; and the striving after a perfectly well-defined end, measurable in mathematical

---

* This aspect of modern capitalism is well put by Kautsky: " One feature of the Middle Ages stands out in marked contrast to our own. In these days the chief object which the capitalist sets before himself is the accumulation of wealth. Your modern capitalist can never have enough money. His great desire is to employ his whole income in amassing capital, expanding his business, undertaking fresh enterprises, or ruining his competitors. After acquiring his first million, he strives for a second, for he fears being outstripped by some rival, and wishes to secure his possessions. The capitalist never employs his whole income for his personal consumption, unless, indeed, he is a fool or a spendthrift, or unless his income is insufficient for his wants." (*Communism in Central Europe*, p. 5.) This last sentence calls to mind Karl Marx's dictum that " the capitalist regards all consumption as a sin against his function."

terms, has encouraged among business people a reckoning, calculating view of life utterly foreign to the hand-to-mouth existence of the peasant or the artist.*

The transition from the old spirit to the new was not violent, but gradual. Weber gives a very good account of how, in a neighbourhood where industry had been conducted for centuries on the traditional basis, one enterprising man would break away from the existing customs and lay the foundations of an industry conducted on modern lines. This change did not entail any great accumulation of capital; all the capital required was subscribed by the man himself out of his savings, aided, possibly, by some contributions by his relatives; what it did require was a new spirit of enterprise and ambition.† It is easy to understand that the capitalist spirit at first asserted itself among the middle

* Weber, *Archiv*, vol. xx., pp. 30-39: " The logical development of Bentham's teaching demanded a simple and single measure of value. The old qualitative measurement of pleasure and pain must give place to a new quantitative measure. This was found in money; in terms of which all human action were thenceforth measured." (Schulze-Gavernitz, *Britischer Imperialismus*, p. 13.) " The capitalist spirit displays an untiring activity, a boundlessness of grasp, quite contrary to the natural impulse to enjoyment and ease, and contentment with the mere necessaries of existence; it makes work and gain an end in themselves, and makes men the slaves of work for work's sake; it brings the whole of life and action within the sphere of an absolutely rationalized and systematic calculation, combines all means to its end, uses every minute to the full, employs every kind of force, and, in alliance with scientific technology and the calculus which unites all these things together, gives to life a clear calculability and abstract exactness." (Troeltsch, *Protestantism and Progress*, pp. 133-4.) Sir William Ashley defines the capitalistic spirit as " the desire of investment for the sake of gain." (*Economic Organization of England*, p. 141.)

† *Archiv*, vol. xx., p. 29.

class in towns, and that the great entrepreneurs and merchant princes who seem to represent it most perfectly to-day were a later development. However, once the breach with tradition was made, and the new spirit of making money for its own sake appeared, the inevitable tendency was for the rich to become richer and the poor poorer; and society has tended more and more during the last 200 years to be divided by a horizontal line into the two classes of possessors and proletariat— the " two nations " of Disraeli's *Sybil*, or the " haves " and " have nots " of vulgar parlance. This tendency has been still further emphasized by the article of the capitalist creed that the maximum productivity is attained only when wages are bad, and that the best preventive of wages rising is the existence of a reserve army of unemployed.*

The pursuit of gain for its own sake having been admitted as the whole duty of man, all artificial barriers in the way of the attainment of this end must naturally be swept away. Sombart, in his excellent book on *The Jews and Modern Capitalism*, indicates as the dominant characteristic of the capitalist age the abolition of all the traditional conventions and understandings that fettered man's industrial life in other centuries. The modest, conservative method of conducting business of the fifteenth and sixteenth centuries, when every detail was regulated by public authorities or by the guilds, gave way, on the approach of capitalism, to the modern methods, based on unlimited competition, unscrupulous underselling, and feverish advertising. The phrase, " business is business," is peculiarly typical of the new spirit. The pre-capitalistic manufacturer or merchant

* Weber, *Archiv*, vol. xx., pp. 23-4.

would have failed to understand why he should be guided by a different code of manners or of morals in his office and in his home.

Naturally, all public restraints which stand in the way of the accumulation of unlimited profit are anathema to men possessed by the capitalist spirit. " Under the influence of *laissez faire*," says Dr. Cunningham, " the functions of government have been reduced to the minimum of securing freedom for the play of individual interests; this is all that the capitalist wishes for at home, and the cosmopolitan capitalist wishes the aid of government to establish in distant lands the sort of order which was maintained in mediæval fairs; his interests are detached from the life of any community; he has no personal part in the country from which his wealth is derived, and his economic activities do not contribute to the wealth of the country in which he lives. He only invokes the spread of a form of civilization, which is little more than a system of police, to provide conditions that are favourable to the pursuit of private interests in planting or in mining. . . ."*

Nor is the modern capitalist restrained by any of the correlative duties which were imposed by the feudal system on property owners as the price they paid for the enjoyment of their rights. Modern capital is essentially a form of property which has not its duties as well as its rights.† The aim of the modern capitalist may be summed up in one word—exploitation; to exploit the undeveloped resources of new countries, to exploit the necessities of the hungry and the defenceless, to exploit the fruits of other people's labour—

---

* *Christianity and Economic Science*, p. 79.
† See Nicolas, *op. cit.*, p. 200.

these are the aims of the business man of the capitalistic era.

All other considerations must give way to the one great aim of money-making. In the following passage Dr. Cunningham draws attention to the disregard of the capitalist for every consideration except his profit: "The capitalist's chief thought is for the security of the fund he possesses, and his next will be for as large an income as may be; these are the points that come before him in investing his capital. His attention is concentrated on the precise bargain he is making and the indirect effects of that bargain are so distant and uncertain that he leaves them out of account, and is ordinarily quite indifferent to them.

"Thus the capitalist is quite indifferent to political considerations in the management of his money. He may be prepared to join in an outcry against the manufacturer who sends improved patterns of guns to a rival power—say, to Russia. But he would feel no scruple in lending his capital to Russia, and thus giving that rival power the means of purchasing the improved arms. There is no great difference between the cases, but he is blind to the possible results of his own action, and thus is indifferent politically.

"Again, the capitalist is indifferent to artistic considerations; the craftsman may have an honest pride in his work, and dislike sending out goods that he feels are not worthy of him; but if there is a public demand for inferior goods, and capital finds that they pay, it will not scruple to cater for a debased taste, and take the profit that accrues.

"In similar fashion it may be said that capital is indifferent to the moral and spiritual welfare of those who are employed; it is clear that the directors of joint stock companies are not legally warranted in spending the money of the shareholders in building churches or schools. And again, capital, as capital, is indifferent to the manner in which land is employed so long as it yields a return. The old-fashioned landlord may have an attachment for his retainers, but the mere speculator is indifferent whether the land produces corn, or sheep, or deer, so long as the investment pays."*

Gain being admittedly the only aim of the capitalist, profit becomes the sole standard of measurement of success or failure in life. In the Middle Ages a transaction would have been judged on the basis of its moral worth and public service, but at the present day the only standard of judgment is the profit which it promises. Thus a strange inversion has taken place. In a capitalistic age, morality itself must submit to be judged on the basis of its tendency to produce a profit or the reverse. Honour is good because it is useful in obtaining credit, punctuality because it helps to render industry efficient, and so on. The whole of modern commercial ethics might be summed up in the phrase: " Honesty is the best policy."†

To the capitalist even religion is to be assessed on a utilitarian valuation. Schulze-Gavernitz gives some amusing examples of the point of view from which religion is regarded by American business men.‡ One of his examples is a letter to Rockefeller from his private secretary, pointing out that the foreign missions should be encouraged because they help to open up new oppor-

---

* *The Use and Abuse of Money*, pp. 46-7.

† Weber, *Archiv*, vol. xx., pp. 15-16. There are some excellent remarks on this in Dean Inge's *Outspoken Essays*, pp. 255-6.

‡ *Op. cit.*, p. 406.

tunities for trade. Mr. Hobson, in his book on *Imperialism*, refers to the " industrial missionary who is designed to plant Christianity upon an ocean of profitable business," and quotes the following passage from a report from the British Consul at Canton: " Immense services might be rendered to our commercial interests, if only the members of the various missions in China would co-operate with our consuls in the exploitation of the country, and the introduction of commercial as well as of purely theological ideas to the Chinese intelligence."

We have now said enough to make it clear what we mean by capitalism, which we have shown to be a particular point of view from which economic activity and gain become ends in themselves, and not merely means to an end. Capitalism has been very justly compared to militarism by Mr. Tawney. The essence of militarism, according to Mr. Tawney, " is not any particular quality or scale of military preparation, but a state of mind which, in its concentration on one particular element in social life, ends finally by exalting it until it becomes the arbiter of all the rest." Capitalism is an exactly analogous state of mind. " What the military tradition and spirit did for Prussia with the result of creating militarism, the commercial tradition and spirit have done for England with the result of creating industrialism." Industrialism—by which term Mr. Tawney means what we have called capitalism— " is no more the necessary characteristic of an economically developed society than militarism is a necessary characteristic of a nation which maintains military forces. It is no more the result of applying science to industry than militarism is the result of the application of science to war; and the idea that it is something

inevitable in a community which uses coal and iron
and machinery, so far from being the truth, is itself a
product of the perversion of mind which industrialism
produces. Men may use what mechanical instruments
they please, and be none the worse for their use. What
kills their souls is when they allow their instruments to
use *them*. The essence of industrialism, in short, is not
any particular method of industry, but a particular
estimate of the importance of industry, which results
in its being thought the only thing that is important at
all, so that it is elevated from the subordinate place
which it should occupy among human interests and
activities into being the standard by which all other
interests and activities are judged."* This description
of what Mr. Tawney calls industrialism is a perfect
description of the phenomenon of " capitalism " which
we have been endeavouring to describe.

The point of view from which men's economic activities are regarded in any age is usually to be found by an
examination of the contemporary dominating economic
theory. Thus, mercantilist notions will probably pre-
vail at a time when the best energy of a country is
directed to the increase of its foreign trade, and physio-
cratic theories when the encouragement of agriculture
is the order of the day. To this rule the age of capitalism forms no exception; the peculiar standpoint from
which industry and commerce are regarded by a capitalistic society is to be learnt from a study of the so-
called liberal or classical political economy, in the
doctrines of which the capitalistic standpoint found at
the same time its expression and its encouragement.
We have seen that the capitalist seeks to confine the

* *Acquisitive Society*, pp. 46-7.

activities of the government within the most narrow limits possible, and it is therefore not surprising to find the classical economists extremely jealous of all government interference. While this jealousy was partly a reaction against the excessive reliance placed by the mercantilists on government assistance, it was at the same time an expression of the desire by the modern business man to employ his resources unfettered so as to produce the maximum benefit to himself.*

Capitalist society, as we have seen, is intensely individualist, and individualism is also one of the distinguishing marks of the classical political economy. Adam Smith followed in the course of the great English and Scottish ethical writers of the early eighteenth century, who, as Hasbach remarks, are extraordinarily rich in expositions of egoism.† Smith was influenced in particular by Hutcheson, who was probably the first philosopher to refer habitually and distinctly to utility as the sole and sufficient measure of virtue, and who did not fall far short of setting up the maxim of absolute economic freedom, by his insistence on the natural right of every man to employ his power according to his pleasure, when the persons or goods of others suffer no disadvantage.‡ It was Bentham who pushed individualism to its fullest extreme by teaching that utilitarianism was the rule to be followed, not only in matters

* Sir William Ashley shows how in this matter "the pressure of business interest went side by side with the elaboration of an abstract social theory." (*The Economic Organization of England,* p. 161.)

† *Untersuchungen über A. Smith in d. Entwickelung d. Politik-ökonomik,* p. 429.

‡ Hasbach, *op. cit.,* p. 425; Leslie Stephen, *English Thought in the Eighteenth Century,* vol. ii., p. 61.

of trade, but in all cases.   In other words, individualism meant, according to Bentham, the same thing in ethics as in political economy.   Since Bentham's time nearly all leading English economists and a large proportion of continental economists have been utilitarians.*   The connection between individualism and the limitation of all government interference was necessary and close. " The principle of individualism," said Louis Blanc, " proclaims *laissez faire* as the maxim of all government."†

One consequence of the introduction of the utilitarian materialist standpoint into economics was that social science came to concern itself far more with production than with either consumption or distribution.   Both under the mercantile system and under the régime of *laissez faire*, production rather than consumption was the topic that received the largest amount of attention.‡ Cardinal Newman heaped invective and contempt upon the dictum of a contemporary economist that " the endeavour to accumulate the means of future subsistence and enjoyment is to the mass of mankind the great source of moral improvement "—a dictum which Newman described as " so very categorical a contradiction of Our Lord, St. Chrysostom, St. Leo, and all the Saints."§   This insistence on the importance of production is, however, quite inevitable in a system of economics dominated by capitalist conceptions, as the fever for an ever-increasing production is one of the

* Bonar, *Philosophy and Political Economy*, pp. 216-8.

† Nicolas, *op. cit.*, p. 246.

‡ Cunningham, *Christianity and Economic Science*, p. 16, and see Ingram, *History of Political Economy*, pp. 108, 225; Villeneuve Bargemont, *Histoire de l'Économie politique*, vol. ii., p. 39.

§ *The Idea of a University*, p. 90.

leading characteristics of the capitalist outlook on life.

The fundamental assumption of classical political economy is the harmony of public and private interests. It had been an old problem with social philosophers whether the interests of men in society were harmonious or antagonistic,* but the classical economists had no hesitation in proclaiming that the true happiness of society could be attained only by allowing the full and unbridled exercise of each individual's selfishness.

The proclamation of this doctrine has been frequently attributed to Adam Smith; but while it is true that he proclaimed, or, rather, assumed it—indeed, it lay at the foundation of all his economics—it must not be forgotten that it had its origin at a much earlier date.† Hobbes introduced the theory that man was moved chiefly by self-interest, and the recognition of self-interest as the starting-point of all political economy and sociology is common to all theories henceforth, until it reached its apex in Adam Smith and Bentham.‡ " Mediæval Catholicism," according to Hermann Levy, " had conceived man as teleologically fitted into a universe created for the Divine purposes. This view

* See Baudrillart, *Études de Philosophie morale*, vol. ii., p. 164.

† Ingram says, " This theory is, of course, not explicitly presented by Smith as a foundation of his economic doctrines, but it is really the secret substratum on which they rest." (*Op. cit.*, p. 91).

‡ " The philosophy of Hobbes, from its close resemblance on many points to the philosophy of Bentham, seems to furnish directly or indirectly many of the premises of what has been called the classical school of modern economics. He regards the world of man as a multitude of competing individuals, whose separate selfish interests lead to an unintended social benefit." (Bonar, *Philosophy and Political Economy*, p. 85.)

was now displaced by the purely naturalistic conception of man as a living machine governed by his own natural though intelligent interest. Quite consistently with the later history of economic thought, the desires of the individual with his particular individual interests are the measure of the greatest possible happiness."* To Shaftesbury and the Deists, self-interest appeared as the indication of the will of God.† An important contribution to this line of thought was made by Mandeville, who, in his *Fable of the Bees*, which bears the significant subtitle *Private Vices, Public Benefits*, makes the point that the greatest friend to society is the man who, by the gratification of luxurious or extravagant tastes, encourages production. According to Mandeville: " He that gives most trouble to thousands of his neighbours, and invents the most operose manufactures, is, right or wrong, the greatest friend to society." Mandeville anticipated the teaching of the later economists that the accumulation of wealth affords the essential material base of all the virtues of civilization.‡

Adam Smith took much of the groundwork of his thought from his English and Scottish predecessors, but he was also considerably influenced by the writings of the Physiocrats. The correct aim of all economic activity, according to this school, was the increase of the *produit net*, and the only way in which a community could be certain of realizing this aim was by allowing all the individuals of which it was composed the fullest freedom to pursue their own private advantage. " By means of this freedom," says Mercier de la Rivière,

* *Economic Liberalism*, pp. 87-8.

† Hasbach, *op. cit.*, p. 174.

‡ Leslie Stephen, *English Thought in the Eighteenth Century* vol. ii , p. 35.

" which is the true element of industry, the desire of enjoyment, stirred up by competition, enlightened by experience and example, is the guarantee that everybody will act always for his own greatest possible advantage, and will consequently contribute to the greatest possible increase of that sum of particular interests, whose reunion forms the general interest of society."*

Adam Smith's importance arose from the fact that he brought together, in support of the maxims of economic freedom, the arguments of many different schools. In Smith, the English philosophers and the Physiocrats came together, and the proposition that the best way to attain to the maximum public benefit was by allowing full freedom of action to individual interests had never before been so ably and convincingly presented.† " The ethical-social foundations of Smith's political economy " according to Hasbach, " may be

* Quoted in Hasbach, *Die Allgemeinen philosophischen Grundlagen*, p. 64. Hasbach says that " economic freedom assumes, in the system of the Physiocrats, the character of a God-willed, immutable law of nature, fixed for all times and places " (*ibid.*, p. 70); and Cliffe Leslie says, " In the Physiocrats the law of nature assumed a theological form—the assumption of a beneficent tendency of the natural desire of man." (*Essays in Moral and Political Philosophy*, p. 167.) Mr. Higgs remarks that: " To maximize the *produit net* was, in their view, to promote the best interests of society, and *vice versa*. An action was, in fact, good or bad, according as it increased or decreased, directly or indirectly, the welfare of society; and they contended that every anti-social action could be shown to diminish the net wealth of society, every laudable action to increase it. From this point of view they would have rejected the ridiculous paradox of Bastiat that the State does harm even when it does good; but they seem, like Adam Smith, to go sometimes dangerously near the doctrine that self-interest is identical with the interest of society as a whole." (*The Physiocrats*, p. 143; Meyer, *Das soziale Naturrecht in der Christlichen Kirche*, p. 37.)

† Hasbach, *Untersuchungen über A. Smith*, etc., p. 423.

explained as a fitting of the teaching of Shaftesbury and Mandeville into the framework of Quesnay's theory of political economy."* In Smith the " mechanical " or " optimistic " view of society reached its fruition. According to this view, man need not consciously aim even at his own happiness or profit; all he has to do is to follow his natural instinct of cupidity, so far as he does not injure any other person; and, inevitably, he will act to the advantage both of himself and of society.† Adam Smith ascribes to the full play of unrestricted competition four advantageous effects: (1) It educates the individual; (2) it reconciles the interests of different classes; (3) it advances individual economy; and (4) it leads to the healthy condition of the general economic organization.‡ The concurrence of individual and social interests is the law of nature, " led by an invisible hand to promote an end which was no part of the intention." " One of the peculiar features of the *Wealth of Nations*," says Buckle, " is to show that, considering society as a whole, it nearly always happens that men, in promoting their own interest, will unintentionally promote the interest of others. Hence, the great practical lesson is not to restrain selfishness, but to enlighten it; because there is a provision in the nature of things by which the selfishness of the individual accelerates the progress of the community. . . . This constant effort . . . is so salutary and powerful that it often secures progress of society in spite of the folly and extravagance of the rulers of mankind. For human institutions are constantly stopping our advance by

* *Allgemeinen Grundlagen*, p. 113.
† Levy, *op. cit.*, p. 90.
‡ Hasbach, *Allgemeinen Grundlagen*, p. 85.

thwarting our natural inclinations."* Selfishness is the
premise of the *Wealth of Nations* ; and man, according
to Smith, is only restrained in the unbridled satisfaction
of his selfishness by sympathy, which is a kind of inverted
selfishness. Selfishness is the great impelling force of
life, which is only kept in check by the regulative force
of sympathy.†

This optimistic view of society, pushed to its logical
conclusion, would lead us to cosmopolitanism. If the
unrestrained pursuit of individual interest is led by an
invisible hand to aid the interest of society, so must the
unrestrained pursuit of national interest lead to the
interest of the whole world. It is for this reason that
the classical economists opposed all restrictive tariffs, and
rejected all so-called " national " systems of political
economy.‡ It would also lead to anarchism, as opposed
to socialism. Thus Godwin, the father of English
socialism, was really an anarchist, because he looked
forward to the day when mankind, urged by an enlightened self-interest, would adopt the one perfect
form of society, without laws or central government.§

We must be careful not to exaggerate the length to
which Adam Smith went in his approval of the pursuit
of one's own gain. The idea that he was a mere
materialist, without any conception of or regard for the
higher purposes of life, is unjust and untenable. Smith

* *History of Civilization*, vol. ii., p. 447.

† Leslie Stephen, *English Thought in the Eighteenth Century*,
vol. ii., p. 321.

‡ Hasbach, *Allgemeinen Grundlagen*, p. 175.

§ " Godwin's theory is the apotheosis of individualism, and
(in a sense) of Protestantism; a purified and enlightened individualism is not to him (as to Rousseau) the beginning, but the
end, of all human progress." (Bonar, *Philosophy and Political
Economy*, p. 203.)

allows that there are many other ends of life besides wealth, but insists that wealth is the only end with which the economist is concerned.   What Smith did then was to isolate this one end of human activity, and to inquire how it could best be attained; and he reached the conclusion that the wealth of society, as well as that of the individuals who compose it, could be best advanced by allowing full freedom to individual efforts and ambitions.   The pursuit of gain, which is the end and aim of all economic activity, is, according to Smith, a matter for private persons and not for governments or rulers; and the presumption is thus against rather than in favour of the interference of the state in economic affairs.*

Nor is it fair to blame Adam Smith for all the evil consequences which resulted from the working of individualism in practice, many of which he could not possibly have foreseen.   It must be remembered that he was on the offensive against an excess of public interference in man's private affairs, and against the obsolete survivals of mercantilism.   The first and most important task of the liberal philosophers of the eighteenth century was to sweep away the existing abuses which flowed from the survival of antiquated institutions; and, if the attack led to consequences which possibly entailed greater social evils than the system attacked, it is not fair to blame those who were concerned to achieve genuine social reforms with the exaggerations of some of their followers.†   According to Leslie Stephen, Smith represents the " calm intellect which has seen through the superstitions of the antiquated restricted

* Bonar, *op. cit.*, p. 175.
† Tawney, *Acquisitive Society*, p. 19.

system, but is not prescient of the troubles that were to come with the bursting of the ancient barriers."*

But, even when all exaggerations are avoided, there is no doubt that the classical school of political economy was at the same time an expression of, and an encouragement to, the modern capitalist idea of society.† The very readiness with which English public opinion assimilated the new doctrines of the economists shows how congenial it found them. Mr. Tawney very justly compares the reception of the idea of economic liberty in England with that of the idea of the rights of man in France; in each case the new idea that attracted was in some way a reflection of the national character.‡ The new philosophy was eagerly seized on by all who wished

* *English Thought in the Eighteenth Century*, vol. ii., p. 325. As Dr. Ingram pointed out: " The mind of Smith was mainly occupied with the work of criticism so urgent in his time; his principal task was to discredit and overthrow the economic system then prevalent, and to demonstrate the radical unfitness of the existing European government to direct the industrial movement. . . . The tendency of the school was undoubtedly to consecrate the spirit of individualism, and the state of non-government. But this tendency, which may with justice be severely condemned in economists of the present time, was then excusable because inevitable. And, whilst it now impedes the work of reconstruction which is for us the order of the day, it then aided the process of social demolition, which was the necessary, though deplorable, condition of a new organization." (*History of Political Economy*, pp. 64, 107.)

† " It has been well said that of philosophic doctrines the saying, ' By their fruits ye shall know them,' is eminently true; and it cannot be doubted that the germs of the vicious methods and false or exaggerated theories of Smith's successors are to be found in his own work, though his good sense and practical bent prevented his following out his principles to their extreme consequences." (Ingram, *op. cit.*, p. 107.)

‡ *Op. cit.*, pp. 16-17.

to justify the pursuit of their own self-interest, and all interference by the state with the freedom of private enterprise could thenceforth be met with a reasoned opposition. In the seventeenth century the state had exercised the right to direct the employment of capital so as to produce the greatest possible national benefit, but, according to the teaching of the classical economists, the only way in which the private capitalist could be trusted to serve the public good was by being left alone to pursue his own advantage.* While the classical school of economics, therefore, did not create the modern spirit of capitalism, it facilitated its growth by providing the doctrine that the transactions most pleasing to the capitalist were at the same time most beneficial to society as a whole.

But, while classical political economy undoubtedly did assist the progress of capitalism in the nineteenth century, it certainly was not the origin of capitalism. No great, widespread, fundamental mental attitude, affecting, at first, a whole nation, and, later, the whole world, has ever had its origin in the disputations of economic professors. Nor do we go to the opposite extreme by suggesting that the classical school of economics arose in order to suit the necessities of a capitalist society. The truth is that the classical school of economics represented in the world of theory what the capitalist spirit represented in the world of practice; while neither was the cause of the other, each aided the other's progress; and both had their origin in the same cause. That brings us to the central point of the inquiry of the present chapter. What was it

* Cunningham, *The Growth of Capitalism in England*, p. 108; and see *The Economic Review*, vol. i., p. 16.

that gave birth to the capitalist spirit in industry ? As
we have said, it was not the classical school of political
economy. Could it then have been the industrial
revolution ? We have already answered this question
in the negative. The capitalist spirit is a point of view,
a state of mind, and is not associated with any particular stage of industrial technique. To say that the
capitalist spirit produced the industrial revolution
would be nearer the truth. The capitalist spirit must
have been the product of some spiritual, interior force.
What was that force ? We suggest that it was Protestantism.

The ideas which we have indicated as characteristic
of the capitalist standpoint are characteristically Protestant ideas—some of them characteristic of Protestantism in general, and some of them peculiar to certain
Protestant creeds. The insistence of the capitalist on
the removal of all restraints by the state is strictly
analogous to the insistence of the Protestant on the
removal of all restraints by the Church. It is private
judgment translated into the realm of industry. We
saw in the last chapter that Protestantism led to the
separation of faith from morals, and to the destruction
of all the sanctions by which a moral life was enforced.
The history of Protestant thought in Great Britain
exactly corroborates what we said on this subject.
" Among the innumerable symptoms " says Buckle, " of
this great movement (towards the weakening of the
ecclesiastical power and the securing of religious liberty)
there were two of peculiar importance. These were the
separation of theology, first from morals, and then from
politics. The separation from morals was effected
late in the seventeenth century; the separation from

politics before the beginning of the eighteenth century."*

Attacks on authority do not, as a rule, end with the defeat of the authority first attacked; and, from the demand for freedom from the interference of the Church in man's economic and social activities, it was an easy step to the demand for freedom from the interference of the state. How could the state refuse to recognize the right of private judgment, when it had been recognized by the Church ? Dr. Cunningham calls attention to the similarity between the attitude of the Presbyterian clergy to the social life of their flocks and the attitude of the classical economists. " The view of economic activities which was taken by Presbyterian ecclesiastics was favourable rather than otherwise to the progress of economic science. They saw no need to interfere with private action in the interests of a Christian standard for the community, and they held that the prudential pursuit of wealth tended to build up a self-disciplined character which was favourable to the formation of sober and godly habits. Adam Smith went a step further, and urged that there was no need in a progressive community for the state to control and direct private

* *History of Civilization*, vol. ii., p. 387. Buckle goes on to remark: " And it is a striking instance of the decline of the old ecclesiastical spirit that both these great changes were begun by the clergy themselves. Cumberland, Bishop of Peterborough, was the first who endeavoured to construct a system of morals without the aid of theology." Whewell says: " It is very remarkable that though Cumberland introduces and repeatedly insists on this aspect of the law of nature as the commands of a divine legislator, he nowhere distinctly fortifies his system by a reference to a future retribution; still less does he aid himself by an appeal to the revealed will and promises of God." (*History of Moral Philosophy*, p. 77.) On the influence of Cumberland on Quesnay, see Hasbach, *Allgemeinen Grundlagen*, pp. 150, 168.

enterprise in the interests of political expediency. He set himself to study the free play of private interests, and argued that there was no need to interfere with it for the benefit of the body politic. The Scottish clergy were not indifferent to Christian duty any more than Adam Smith was indifferent to the increase of national power; but they held that it was unnecessary either for one object or the other to interfere with the private freedom of individuals in the conduct of their own affairs."* The tendency for the Church in England to stand aside from the regulation of the economic and social activities of its members was greatly strengthened by the rise of nonconformism at the end of the eighteenth century. Methodism was extremely individualist in character. It laid the greatest emphasis on the direct intercourse between the individual and his Creator, and attached very little importance to corporate action or to society, whether ecclesiastical or civil. Methodism, according to Troeltsch, represented the revival of ancient Christendom in a totally individualistic form.†

* *Christianity and Economic Science*, pp. 71-72; *Property, Its Duties and Rights*, p. 140.

† *Soziallehren*, p. 836. One sign of the growing tendency of the Church to be divorced from the affairs of everyday business life was the development of a hitherto unheard-of theory that a different standard of morality could be applied in business and in private life. Defoe, in *The Complete Tradesman*, lays stress on the necessity of man's keeping his religious and his business life apart, and in not allowing one to interfere with the other. " There is some difference between an honest man and an honest trades-man. . . . There are some latitudes, like poetical licences in other cases, which a tradesman must be and is allowed, and which by the custom and usage of a trade he may give himself a liberty in, which cannot be allowed in other cases to any men, no, nor to the tradesman himself out of his business." (*The Complete Tradesman*, 1819 Edn., pp. 17, 55. See *Property, Its Duties and Rights*, p. 141 *n.*)

As the result of this double tendency—for the Church to stand aside from the social and economic life of its members, and of the state to refrain from interfering in any way with the private enterprise of individuals—the old idea of a corporate social life had almost disappeared by the end of the eighteenth century, its place being taken by the new conception of the infallibility of the enlightened and intelligent pursuit of the self-interest of the individual. The natural free-play of private ambitions and desires had replaced the old institutions of Church and state as the machinery by which the maximum social benefit could be achieved.* The new mechanical-optimistic ideas of the natural working out of man's pursuit of his own self-interest for the public good was itself a kind of religion in the early nineteenth century; it was the creed that was admitted to rule man in his social relationships; just as Christianity—of one sort or another—was admitted to rule man in his spiritual relationships. The existence of an independent body of social or economic ethics side by side with institutions claiming to be Christian Churches is a phenomenon which could appear only when the latter had ceased to assert the infallibility of their moral teaching, and when the sanctions by which they had enforced that teaching had been relaxed. In a word, it was a phenomenon peculiar to Protestantism.

The second great characteristic of capitalism to which we drew attention is its individualism, and here, also, we recognize a characteristic of Protestantism. The mediæval Church insisted very strongly on the organic, corporate nature of Christianity. The doctrine of the communion of saints taught that the Church was com-

* Tawney, *op. cit.*, p. 12; Levy, *Economic Liberalism*, p. 90.

posed not merely of the living faithful, but also of the departed, whether in Purgatory or in Heaven; and, further, that all these different classes of members of the Church could help each other by their prayers. The teaching on supererogatory works and indulgences also tended to foster a strong sense of solidarity. The Reformation, on the other hand, was intensely individualist. The doctrine of private judgment naturally led to a strongly individualistic character, which the leaders of the movement were unable to keep within the bounds they would have desired. It has been truly said that the individualistic spirit of the Reformation neutralized where it did not mould the teaching of the reformers.*

The ancient idea of solidarity was also dealt a shattering blow by the doctrine of justification by faith alone. With the rejection of works, as capable of aiding in the process of justification, the whole Catholic teaching on the communion of saints, on supererogatory works, and on indulgences, naturally fell to the ground; and the old organic, social conception of Christian life was replaced by one of the lonely striving of each individual for his own salvation. Troeltsch says that the Reformation completely destroyed the organic conception of the mediæval Church;† and Louis Blanc said that modern individualism had been inaugurated by Luther.‡ Weber draws attention to the lonely—almost desolate—note which is to be found in the literature of the Puritans, which is full of warnings against placing any reliance

* Gooch, *English Democratic Ideas in the Seventeenth Century*, p. 1.
† *Soziallehren*, p. 551.
‡ Nicolas, *op. cit.*, p. 246. See also Baudrillart, *Jean Bodin et son Temps*, p. 30.

on the help and friendship of other men.* Possibly the greatest example in literature of the conception of the lonely journey of man to the goal of his salvation is Bunyan's *Pilgrim's Progress*, on which Professor Dowden makes the following illuminating comment: "All that is best and most characteristic in Bunyan proceeds from that inward drama, in which the actors were three—God, Satan, and a solitary human soul. If external influences from events or men affected his spirit, they came as nuncios or messengers from God or from the Evil One. Institutions, Churches, ordinances, rites, ceremonies, could help him little, or not at all. The journey from the City of Destruction to the Celestial City must be undertaken on a special summons by each man for himself alone; if a companion join him on the way, it lightens the trials of the road; but, of the companions, each one is an individual pilgrim, who has started on a great personal adventure, and who, as he enters the dark river, must undergo his particular experiences of hope or fear."† This conception of the inability of any man to help his fellows on their spiritual progress is profoundly antipathetic to Catholic conceptions of life; it is, at the same time, strongly individualistic and characteristically Protestant.

There is no need to labour the point that Protestantism is individualist, because this is admitted on all sides, both by Catholic and Protestant writers. Cardinal Gasquet says that individualism became the " dominant philosophy " of the new era following the Reformation;‡ and Villeneuve Bargemont sees in the Reformation

---

* *Archiv*, vol. xxi., pp. 11-13.
† *Puritan and Anglican*, p. 234.
‡ *Henry VIII. and the English Monasteries*, p. 474.

a reversion to antique epicureanism—" the moral of personal interest."* Dr. Westcott says that the Reformation " was the affirmation, final and decisive; it was, I had almost said, in the order of Providence, the revelation of individuality ";† and Beer states that, after the Reformation, society, as a whole, moved towards individualism, " whose first manifestation was the Elizabethan age—an age of pioneers, men of keen initiative."‡

From religious individualism, the passage was easy to political and social individualism.§ It is only natural that men who have been taught to rely on their own private judgment in matters of faith, and on their own lonely efforts to attain salvation, should resent dictation and hindrances in their political and economic life. One's standpoint towards religion naturally colours one's standpoint towards every other human activity. " Individualist in their faith," says Mr. Tawney of the English nonconformists, " they were individualist in their interpretation of social morality."‖ Individualism is a quality that cannot be confined to any one department of man's life; and it is only reasonable to expect

* *Histoire d'Économie politique*, vol. i., p. 318.
† *Social Aspects of Christianity*, p. 121.
‡ *History of British Socialism*, vol. i., p. 46. It is Mr. H. G. Wood's opinion that " Dissent tended to embrace an extreme form of individualism " (*Property, Its Duties and Rights*, p. 145 *n.*), and see the article on *Christianity and Economics* in Palgrave's *Dictionary of Political Economy ;* Stang, *Socialism and Christianity*, p. 104; Troeltsch, *Soziallehren*, p. 948; Marshall, *Principles of Economics*, 5th Edn., p. 742; Ingram, *op. cit.*, p. 33.
§ " The Reformation had a positive and a negative side; the negative side was the spiritual and civil freeing of the individual." (Schulze-Gavernitz, *op. cit.*, p. 9; and see Hasbach, *Allgemeinen Grundlagen*, p. 31.)
‖ *Op. cit.*, p. 229.

that men who have been trained to be individualist in one thing should become individualist in all. It is difficult to resist the conclusion that the individualism of the Reformation and the individualism of the capitalist spirit had some connection. It is more than a coincidence that these two phenomena should have appeared with the most marked intensity in the same community, and that the country which carried Protestantism to its furthest extreme in one century should have carried capitalism to its furthest extreme in the next.*

Two features, therefore, of the orthodox political economy, which was the expression of the capitalist spirit—the jealousy of all government restraint, and the individualist point of view—we have discovered also in Protestantism, and we must now inquire how far the third feature which we named—namely, the idea that the full unfettered freedom of every individual to pursue his private interests led, " as by an invisible hand," to the realization of the common good—had a Protestant foundation.   In order to obtain a satisfactory answer to this problem, it is necessary for us to say a few words

* See Levy, *Economic Liberalism*, p. 86 *n*.   Sir William Ashley says: " The Reformation in religion, whether for good or for ill, was an expression of individualism; it emphasized the direct relation to God of the individual soul.   But religious individualism was but a part or aspect of a universal tendency in the direction of freeing the individual from tradition and usage, and stimulating him to think and act for himself.   And this took shapes both good and bad; it showed itself in greater individual enterprise, and improved methods of production, and showed itself in more obvious selfishness and self-seeking; what contemporary writers call ' private affection,' ' private profit,' and ' singular lucre.' In all the economic relations of human beings with one another it meant more of what we now call ' competition,' and all that it involves." (*The Economic Organization of England*, p. 64.)

about the distinctive contribution which was made to social conceptions by Calvinism. In dealing with this matter we must acknowledge our indebtedness to Professor Max Weber, whose invaluable papers in the *Archiv für Sozialwissenschaft und Sozialpolitik* opened up the discussion for the first time, have stood the test of much hostile criticism, and remain to-day the classical authority on the subject. It is impossible to consider any point relating to the influence of Calvinism on capitalism without deriving assistance from Professor Weber's research and suggestive criticism.

We have already referred to the contrast between the social tendencies of Lutheranism and Calvinism. Lutheranism was, in its economic outlook, scarcely removed at all from the Middle Ages, and it derived its social importance from the indirect results of its theological doctrines rather than from any distinctively new social ideas that it professed. Luther's violence against usury, his preference for agriculture, his prejudice against competition, and his desire for fixed prices, all show him to have been a conservative, if not a reactionary, in the economic field. He regarded economics from the consumer's standpoint, and would have desired, if it were possible, a static society ruled by the overseeing care of the prince. Far from encouraging the development of capitalistic enterprise or urban industries, he waged fierce war on the growing industrialism of his time. In this, as in all other economic respects, Luther stood much nearer to the Middle Ages than to the present day.*

Calvin's economic ideas were more advanced. He

* Troeltsch, *Soziallehren*, pp. 571-84; Schmoller, *op. cit.*, pp. 491 *et seq.*

lay less under mediæval influences, and took a more independent view. He had not Luther's prepossession in favour of agriculture, and he attacked the whole basis of the teaching on usury.* It is, nevertheless, important to avoid exaggerating Calvin's personal advance on the prevailing ideas of his time. When speaking of Calvinism as an influence on social life and thought, we must bear in mind that Calvin did not foresee all the consequences of his teaching, and that many of the most important social consequences of Calvinism were the indirect result of the Calvinistic teaching on theological points. For one thing, Calvin was not nearly so enthusiastic about the development of industries in Geneva as is sometimes stated by his modern admirers. It is true that he had not Luther's prejudice against industries and urban life in general, and that he encouraged the introduction of new manufactures among his followers; but he would have had no sympathy with the monster scale industries of to-day, and he poured abuse on the great commercial towns of his time—Venice and Antwerp. Above all, with Calvin, commerce and industry would have to take their place in strict subordination to religion.† Moreover, Calvinists in the first century of their existence had no sympathy with speculation and the methods of " getting rich quick " so familiar to the modern capitalist.‡ Indeed, it is a mistake to associate early Calvinism with urban industry or urban ways of life at all. Its connection with the French nobility inculcated a different idea of life, and

* Erhardt in *Theologische Studien und Kritiken*, 1880, pp. 128 *et seq.;* Stern, *Socialisten der Reformationszeit*, p. 11.

† Kampschulte, *Johann Calvin*, vol. i., p. 430; Troeltsch, *Soziallehren*, p. 706.

‡ Levy, *Economic Liberalism*, p. 60.

it was not till after the fall of the Huguenots that it was driven to the towns. After this the Calvinist idea of society became urban, and was fully developed in the Netherlands, in England, and in America.

The oldest Calvinism was highly aristocratic, and, far from encouraging any egalitarian ideas, it attached considerable importance to the due observance of distinctions of rank and dignity, in which it was aided by the teaching on predestination. The strict regard which was paid to rank and dignity in Geneva may be seen from the luxury ordinances or sumptuary regulations, which prescribed a carefully graded mode of life for every class of citizen.* Moreover, while Calvinism, like every other variety of Protestantism, was necessarily individualistic in its essence, anything in the nature of the modern *laissez faire* idea of society would have been abhorrent to the first Calvinists, who did not see the full implications of their teaching. The society which Calvin founded in Geneva was animated by a kind of Christian socialism, not in the modern sense of the word, but in the sense that it was hoped to rule the whole life of the city and of society according to a Christian solidarity, and to work out God's will on earth through the medium of Calvinist institutions. Calvinism largely adopted the social policy of the Middle Ages, animated by the guild spirit, and with regulations for the control and direction of commerce and industry. The innumerable interferences with private enterprise authorized by the Genevan institutions are as alien as possible to the spirit of *laissez faire*.† Even in England, the early

* Troeltsch, *Soziallehren*, pp. 656, 964; Kampschulte, *Johann Calvin*, vol. ii., p. 351.

† Troeltsch, *Soziallehren*, pp. 642, 667-8; Choisy, *L'Etat chrétien*, pp. 117, 121, 244 and *passim*.

Protestants sought merely to remedy the evils of existing society by bringing it, as they thought, more into conformity with the injunctions of scripture, which, on this matter, as on all others, was regarded as the infallible guide.*

Calvinism, therefore, so far as social and economic affairs were concerned, did not create any violent revolution, nor did it make any sudden break with the past. There was nothing in the social or economic teaching of Calvin to account for the undoubted fact that, in later years, the social and economic complexion of Calvinist communities assumed a very different hue from that of Lutheran. We need not labour what is really a commonplace to-day—namely, that in the seventeenth and eighteenth centuries Calvinists came to be identified more and more with the commercial and industrial types of society, while Lutheranism and Catholicism tended to be identified rather with the more old-fashioned mode of life. That this was so is admitted by everybody, and, indeed, cannot be denied.† What concerns us here is to try to discover why this was so.

As we have already said more than once in the preceding pages, the social and economic consequences of the Reformation were the result, not of any peculiar views on social matters held by the reformers themselves, but of certain of their theological doctrines. This is as true of the different denominations of Protestantism as it is of Protestantism considered as a whole; and, therefore, if we wish to discover the causes which

* Cunningham, *Christianity and Economic Science*, pp. 60-61.
† Troeltsch, *Soziallehren*, passim ; Schulze-Gavernitz, *op. cit.*, pp. 51, 63-4.

led to the development of quite different types of society among later Lutherans and later Calvinists, we must seek for the germ of this development in the theological teaching of the founders of these creeds. There is no doubt that neo-Lutheranism and neo-Calvinism inculcated different virtues, and pointed out different roads to perfection; the former attached more importance to the passive virtues of submission, patience, and obedience, and the latter to the active virtues of energy, enterprise, and independence. According to Troeltsch: " The development of the two confessions is opposed. Lutheranism has become in Germany the advocate of the conservative, aristocratic ordering of life, and develops in its followers the Christian virtues of interior piety detached from the world, as well as those of resignation, piety, patience, and perseverance. Calvinism, on the other hand, tends to the accentuation of democratic and liberal thought, and develops the virtues of independence and freedom. . . . Neo-Calvinism demands the Christian-liberal ordering of the state and of society, and the independence and freedom of the individual. . . . Throughout, it believes in the Christian ideal of freedom. The patriarchal and conservative elements of Christian ethics are pushed into the background, and the liberal social-reform ethic is placed in the foreground."* " Lutheranism " says Schulze-Gavernitz, " taught submission and patience; Calvinism taught action. . . . Lutheranism aimed at supporting, Calvinism at breaking down, privileges."† It is easy enough to see how the possession of such different ideals, and the insistence on such different virtues, would lead to the formation of distinct types of society

* *Soziallehren*, pp. 790-2.   † *Op. cit.*, pp. 51, 63-4.

among the adherents of the two creeds. It is obvious that the Calvinistic virtues are precisely those which would be most highly appreciated in a society animated by the capitalist spirit; and, further, that a society holding such views on the importance of enterprise, energy, and activity would probably develop the peculiar outlook which we have described as capitalistic. What concerns us here, however, is to inquire how far the characteristic tone of what we have called Neo-Calvinism can be shown to be a development of the original Calvinist teaching. In other words, we must inquire which of the theological doctrines of Calvin it was that contained the germ which afterwards developed into the peculiar liberal, individualist, active attitude towards life of later Calvinism; and how this development took place.

The solution of this problem is Max Weber's most valuable contribution to economic history. He has demonstrated beyond denial that the germ of the later Calvinist liberalism is to be found in the doctrines of predestination and of the indestructibility of justification, and, in particular, in the signs by which the justified might be recognized. The last-mentioned subject is of especial importance, because it introduces us to the peculiarly Protestant idea of intramundane asceticism, which undoubtedly played a most important part in forming the Protestant character. This intramundane asceticism, as distinguished from the mediæval or Catholic idea of monastic asceticism, was characterized by two great ideals—one, the leading of a sober, frugal, industrious life, and the other, the unremitting, indefatigable pursuit of one's worldly calling. By these marks could be distinguished the elect and the justified, and by such conduct could the Christian glorify God, and prove the fact of his own redemption.

The insistence on the pursuit of one's worldly calling attained an importance in Protestantism that it had never attained in Catholicism. It must not be supposed, however, that the Catholic Church in the Middle Ages had in any way disparaged the dignity of all legitimate professions and trades, or, still less, that it had ever connived at laziness or sloth in the occupations by which men earned their livelihood. On the contrary, St. Augustine's strongly expressed views on the dignity of labour were universally accepted in the Middle Ages.* Where the difference arose in the Catholic and Protestant points of view was in the rejection by the latter of the distinction between the domain of nature and the domain of grace, and the consequent disappearance of the Catholic idea of the supernatural vocations. In the Catholic system, the highest vocations had been regarded as those which called the Christian to lead a life upon the supernatural plane, while the natural vocations merely tended to the perfection of man on the natural plane. The duty of diligence in one's natural vocation was insisted upon quite as emphatically by the Catholic as by the Protestant; but the latter regarded the natural vocation as the only vocation open to man. It consequently attained a position of importance among Protestants which it had never attained among Catholics.

* Cunningham, *Christianity and Economic Science.* pp. 26-8; Grisar, *Life of Luther*, vol. iv., p. 128; Paulus, " Die Wertung der weltlichen Beruf im Mittelalter," in *Historische Jahrbuch*, 1911; Antoine, *Cours d'Économie sociale*, p. 159; Sabatier, *L'Eglise et le Travail manuel ;* Champagny, *La Bible et l'Économie politique*, p. 210; O'Brien, *Essay on Mediæval Economic Teaching*, pp. 137, 223.

Luther's rejection of the distinction between the domain of nature and the domain of grace led naturally to a new conception of the importance of the worldly callings. "The Middle Ages," according to Troeltsch, "had closely connected the lower kinds of temporal labour with the spiritual riches of the Church, but the connection was potential and prospective only, and required to be amplified by purely religious service. Nor was it binding on the lords of religious life, the representatives and exemplars of the truest Christian feeling. Protestantism first identified grace and nature by teaching that work in this world was given by the will of God, and by making it the normal and necessary test of each man's state of grace."* Weber points out that the word *beruf*, or calling, when used in the German translations of the Bible, was imbued with the spirit of the translator, and not with that of the author; and that the word is found used in its modern sense only in post-Reformation literature. He further suggests that the use of the English word "calling," in its modern sense, may be traced to Cranmer's translation of the Bible.† This conception of the all-important duty of the fulfilment of the worldly calling led to the peculiarly Protestant idea of intramundane asceticism, which, according to Weber, is to be distinguished from the old Catholic asceticism by three traits: (1) the rejection of all irrational means of asceticism; (2) the abandonment of contemplation; and (3) the leading of an ascetic life in business and in the family.‡

The idea of the "calling" did not, however, attain its full importance in Lutheranism. Although Luther

* *Soziallehren*, p. 652.   † *Archiv*, vol. xx., pp. 35-41.
‡ *Archiv*, vol. xxxi., p. 590; Schmoller, *op. cit.*, pp. 478, 485.

was led to emphasize the importance of intramundane asceticism by his abolition of the distinction between nature and grace, and by his undying hatred of the monastic life and its counsels of perfection, he rather kept in the background the idea that the fulfilment of one's calling could be a proof or testimony of justification. In this he was no doubt influenced by his constant fear of giving countenance to anything that might be accused of savouring of the doctrine of justification by works; and he consequently was inclined to represent the fulfilment of one's calling as a divinely ordained task or dispensation, which men pleased God by performing dutifully.* In this, as in other respects, Lutheranism was a conservative rather than a progressive force, and it was left for the more logical Calvinists to work out Luther's doctrines to their proper conclusions. The conception of the calling, as held by Lutheranism, was closely bound up with the feudal, conservative society organized on a class system, which tended to keep each person in his own class. In other words, as we said above, the Lutheran conception of society was static, and the conception of the calling was consequently coloured by the same idea. " The Lutheran attitude towards life," says Troeltsch, " was as far as possible from giving an initial impulse to the mighty upward movement of modern economic life."†

It was Calvinism that took the forward step that gave to the idea of intramundane asceticism its later overwhelming importance. This it did by providing a definite and valuable reward for the person who fulfilled his calling. Luther had pointed to no particular reward

* Weber, *Archiv*, vol. xx., pp. 41-50.
† *Protestantism and Progress*, p. 130.

for the fulfilment of one's calling, and, indeed, his teaching on the uselessness of works rather pointed to the non-existence of any such reward; and, amongst Catholics, the greater rewards were attributed to other kinds of works.   Calvinism recognized the fulfilment of one's calling, and the leading of a life generally conformable to the maxims of intramundane asceticism, as the sign of one's election to salvation.   This new idea invested the calling with an altogether unprecedented importance.*   The development of this new conception was to some extent the logical outcome of the Calvinist teaching on the indestructibility of grace.   According to Calvinism, the man who is once justified is always justified, and he need not strain his faculties to retain the new grace-born state, but must publish it to the world.   The manner best calculated to prove the fact of one's regeneration to oneself, and to publish it to the world, is by leading a life of intramundane asceticism, and by fulfilling the duties of one's calling.†

The earliest Calvinists did not believe that there could be any outward distinction between the chosen and the rejected, but, as the popular creed developed, it came to be believed that a man's spiritual regeneration could be testified to by the manner of his life.   It was taught that incessant activity in one's vocation dispelled religious doubt, and assured one of the possession of the state of grace.‡   The new Protestant conception of the state of grace was to belong to the elect, and the only way in which this association could be proved was by the systematic mode of conducting one's life, and by the

* Weber, *Archiv*, vol. xxxi., pp. 583-4.
† Troeltsch, *Soziallehren*, p. 623.
‡ Weber, *Archiv*, vol. xxi., pp. 19-20; Levy, *op. cit.*, p. 77.

avoidance of all indolence and inactivity.* The Catholic
Church taught the possibility of the gradual accumulation of grace by individual good works, but the Calvinist
conception of the state of grace demanded a persevering,
systematic course of conduct, by which a man's spiritual
condition could be recognized by the whole world. The
judge of one's spiritual health was not, as in Catholicism,
a confessor, but one's own neighbours.† It is easy to
understand how this conception would lead to a new
kind of spiritual aristocracy, an aristocracy of the
diligent, the active, and the zealous—the " saints "—
instead of the old aristocracy of the monks. It is also
easy to see how it might lead to a close connection
between a man's religious reputation and his worldly
success. To be excluded from the category of the
elect in a community where such ideas prevailed would
be a stigma to be avoided at all costs. Weber draws
attention to the practice in some Baptist communities
in the United States, in which business men desire to
be admitted to baptism, because they know that the
fact that they get through the moral examination which
is held before baptism is administered will act as a kind
of guarantee of their business credit; and further calls
attention to the indisputable fact that, when the religious
life disappears from capitalist communities, recourse is
had to all sorts of clubs, confederations, fellowships, and
other organizations to take the place of the old organized
religious opinion as the tests of public respectability.‡

* Weber, *Archiv*, vol. xxi., p. 73.

† Weber, *Archiv*, vol. xxi., pp. 25-7; vol. xxxi., p. 584.

‡ *Archiv*, vol. xxxi., pp. 586-7. In Rowntree's book on
Quakerism we meet the following characteristic remark: " Real
piety favours the success of a trader by insuring his integrity and
fostering habits of prudence and forethought—important items

The Calvinist teaching on the importance of leading a life of intramundane asceticism, and, amongst other things, of fulfilling one's vocation, may seem to approximate to the Catholic teaching on the importance of works for justification.   But this is not really the case. While it is true that Calvinists never showed the same abhorrence as Lutherans to admitting works to have some share in the process of justification, it must be remembered that the ideal life of asceticism was not meant to serve as an aid to justification, but as the proof of a justification already accomplished, and, moreover, that the kind of works admired by the Calvinists was much narrower than, and very different from, that admired by Catholics.   The latter attached great weight to sacrifices, sacraments, and other purely spiritual works, whereas the Calvinists attached importance only to intramundane asceticism and the fulfilment of one's calling.   It is possibly correct to say that the Catholics advocated works, and the Calvinists work.*

The work thus advocated by the Calvinists was not intended as an aid to justification; indeed, the idea of the creature playing any part in his own justification was necessarily excluded from a system based on predestination.   It was advocated, in the first place, because it was a sign or mark by which the chosen might be assured of their own election, and might be recognized by the world as being among the justified, and, in the second place, because it was held to glorify God.   The Catholic had many means at his disposal with which to glorify

---

in obtaining that standing and credit in the commercial world, which is requisite for the steady accumulation of wealth." (Quoted in Levy's *Economic Liberalism*, p. 59.)

* Weber, *Archiv*, vol. xxi., pp. 21-3.

God, but the Protestant had nothing but his ascetic life and the fulfilment of his vocation.* Calvinists believed that work of this kind glorified God by realizing the potential capacities of the Universe which He had designed for His own glorification,† and they consequently taught that incessant activity and energy could not but be pleasing to God.‡ Sir William Petty said of the leaders of the Dutch War of Freedom: "Dissenters of this kind are for the most part sober-thinking and patient men, and such as believe that labour and industry is their duty towards God."§ "It is for action," we read in Baxter's *Christian Directory*, "that God maintaineth us and our activities; work is the moral as well as the natural end of power. . . . It is action that God is most served and honoured by."‖ "The Puritan" according to Schulze-Gavernitz, "held unshakeably to the irreconcilable opposition between good and evil. The aim of human life to him was not an agreeable balance book or the greatest good of the greatest number, but the Kingdom of God. The other world is the ultimate end; but, in opposition to the Middle Ages, he carried this other world over into this world; he did not seek salvation in fleeing the world, but in glorifying God *in* the world."¶

The fulfilment of one's vocation was the principal constituent of the intramundane asceticism, which was, as we have seen, the Calvinist ideal of Christian conduct. But we must not forget that the ideal asceticism of the Calvinist included other elements as well. It was dis-

---

* Weber, *Archiv*, vol. xx., p. 41.   † *Ibid.*, vol. xxi., p. 17.
‡ Troeltsch, *Soziallehren*, p. 622.
§ Weber, *Archiv*, vol. xxx., p. 184.
‖ Weber, *Archiv*, vol. xxi., p. 76.   ¶ *Op. cit.*, p. 27.

tinguished by a sober, methodical, frugal method of life, with the avoidance of all display and luxury. The virtue of magnificence, which was so highly praised in the Middle Ages, was not recognized by the Calvinists, who favoured instead an austere, saving existence. "The Protestants," according to Sombart, "had lost all sense of beauty; *magnificentia* found no place in their ethical and religious system, well-suited as it was to their cold, drab, whitewashed, pictureless kirks. . . . Indeed, in Puritan ethics, the very opposite of *magnificentia*, miserliness, became one of the cardinal virtues."*

In the last sentence, and in other portions of the present chapter, we have used the word " Puritan " as if it were synonymous with " Calvinist." We make no apology for doing so, because it was in the peculiar British variety of Calvinism known as Puritanism that all the Calvinist doctrines we have been discussing reached their fullest development, and exercised their most powerful influence on social life and thought. Though the idea of the importance of fulfilling one's vocation was common to all ascetic Protestantism, it found its highest expression in English Puritanism.† In the sense in which we use the word, we mean by Puritanism the peculiar brand of Protestantism which prevailed among the non-episcopal Calvinists in England and Holland. Strictly speaking, this is a misuse of the

---

* *Quintessence of Capitalism*, p. 259.

† *Archiv*, vol. xxi., p. 74. " The highest and most perfect expression of Calvinism is Puritanism; so it was in its origin, and so it remains to this day." (Batault, *Le Problème juif*, p. 182.) " Puritanism," according to Mr. H. G. Wood, " is rightly regarded as the most representative interpretation of Protestant morality amongst English-speaking peoples." (*Property, Its Duties and Rights*, p. 136; Conrad Noel, *Socialism and Church History*, p. 224.)

term, because Puritanism in the strict sense refers to a particular section of English reformed opinion, not necessarily outside the established Church; and Puritanism, in this sense, disappeared in the middle of the seventeenth century, its place being taken by Dissent.* But Puritanism has come to bear in general usage a much wider meaning than this, and it now stands for the particular form of Dutch and English Protestantism which prevailed outside the established church after the middle of the seventeenth century.†

Puritanism in this sense represented the meeting-point of Calvinism and Anabaptism, and contained elements from each of these creeds.‡ But, in spite of the many elements which went to its composition, Puritanism was animated by a single code of ethics, in which the duty of leading a life of intramundane asceticism and the fulfilment of one's calling occupied a prominent place.§ Troeltsch indicates as characteristic features of Puritanism: " The demand for ascetic conduct and of work-activity as the best means of spiritual and corporal discipline . . . the utmost simplicity of life with regard to clothing and comfort; the

* Douglas Campbell, *The Puritan in Holland, England, and America*, vol. ii., pp. 238, 399.

† Puritan is defined by Weber as: " The ascetically-directed religious movements of the seventeenth century in England and Holland, without distinction of the programme as to Church forms and dogma, and influenced by the Independents, Congregationalists, Baptists, Mennonites, and Quakers." (*Archiv*, vol. xxi., p. 2); and by Schulze-Gavernitz as: " All the religious movements of the seventeenth century which were outside the episcopal Church." (*Op. cit.*, p. 27.)

‡ Weber, *Archiv*, vol. xxi., p. 2; Batault, *op. cit.*, p. 176; Meyer, *Das Soziale Naturrecht in der christlichen Kirche*, pp. 31-2; Troeltsch, *Soziallehren*, p. 817.

§ Weber, *Archiv*, vol. xxi., pp. 3 and 45.

practical capacity, assurance, and honour in all callings, which lead to a very practical social, political, and business activity."* The Quakers, who differed in many respects from the Calvinists, were at one with the Puritans in their insistence on intramundane asceticism as the sign of election. According to them, the only way in which the regenerated could be recognized was by the life which they led.† The Puritan ideals of asceticism were also held by the Methodists.‡

It is impossible to exaggerate the influence which must have been exercised over the English people by this great religious manifestation, which was the most powerful spiritual influence in England from the middle of the seventeenth to the middle of the nineteenth century, and which coloured, for good or evil, all English thought. " To thousands of Englishmen," says Gardiner, " Puritanism was the very gospel itself, the voice of God speaking to a careless generation;"§ and we read elsewhere: " No one can understand the sources

* *Soziallehren*, p. 776.

† Weber, *Archiv*, vol. xxi., p. 68. Troeltsch says that the Quakers shared the same ideals with regard to asceticism and the fulfilment of one's vocation that had been held in Geneva, but that they were based on the ground of freewill. (*Soziallehren*, p. 913.) In their complete rejection of the interference of the state, the Quakers were the direct forerunners of the Manchester School. (Schulze-Gavernitz, *op. cit.*, p. 17.)

‡ Lecky, *England in the Eighteenth Century*, vol. iii., pp. 86-9; Conrad Noel, *Socialism and Church History*, p. 244. Weber says that the place of the vocation is the same in Methodism as in Calvinism (*Archiv*, vol. xxi., p. 61), and Troeltsch, that Puritanism reappeared at the end of the eighteenth century under the form of Methodism. (*Soziallehren*, p. 778.) Wesley's sermons contain numerous observations very characteristic of seventeenth-century Puritanism. (See *Property, Its Duties and Rights*, pp. 151 *et seq.*)

§ *The Great Civil War*, vol. i., p. 31.

of our mixed civilization without studying the great Puritanical movement of the seventeenth century. It is necessary to penetrate to the heart of this movement and find some sympathetic point of connection with it, before we can appreciate some of the most powerful influences which have moulded the English people, and made them what they are."* " Puritanism," according to Troeltsch, " became the moral school of the English middle-class;"† and Schulze-Gavernitz says that " Puritanism coloured the point of view of a whole nation, just as Catholicism had coloured the Middle Ages."‡

One aspect of the influence of Puritanism cannot fail to attract attention—namely, that, wherever Puritanism flourished, trade and industry flourished also. We have already drawn attention to the fact that the early Calvinists had not the same antipathy to industrial pursuits as had the early Lutherans, and the whole history of Calvinism, especially in its Puritanical form, shows that Calvinists were always prepared to encourage trade and industry. Weber remarks that most of the shining lights of Calvinism arose from the mercantile classes, and that among Calvinists business ability and

* Tulloch, *English Puritanism*, p. 1.
† *Soziallehren*, p. 777.
‡ *Op. cit.*, p. 27. " The long-enduring and deep-seated strength of Puritanism may be gauged by the success that always attends appeals made to it in the present day by time-serving politicians and popularity-hunting journalists." (Morris and Bax, *Socialism, Its Growth and Outline*, p. 97.) It must be remembered that the peculiarly Puritan point of view spread outside the ranks of the Puritans themselves, and coloured the attitude towards life of other denominations. (Troeltsch, *op. cit.*, pp. 709 and 789.) On the influence of Puritanism generally, see Seebohm, *The Era of the Protestant Reformation ;* Thorold Rogers, *The Economic Inter-pretation of History*, p. 83.

piety have always gone together.*   It is a commonplace
that Calvinist immigrants have always been considered
of value from the industrial point of view, and the
business success of certain Puritanical sects—the
Quakers in England and America, and the Mennonites
in Germany and the Netherlands—is notorious.†   In
England, ever since the seventeenth century, the world
of business has been closely connected with the world of
Puritanism.   Hermann Levy quotes numerous extracts
from seventeenth-century writers to show how early
this connection became remarkable, and concludes that:
" It may be accepted as certain that even at the
beginning of the seventeenth century the importance
of Dissent in the most prosperous trades had attracted
general attention."‡   The Pilgrim Fathers brought the
Calvinist tradition to America, where, in course of time,
the urban industrial spirit of the northern states became
dominant over the conservative, agricultural spirit of
the south.§

This connection cannot have been purely accidental,
and it is important that we should understand how it
arose.   It is sometimes suggested that the Puritans
turned to trade because they had been excluded from
other pursuits.   Thus Douglas Campbell says that it
was owing to the penal laws excluding Puritans from
Parliament, from the learned professions, and from the
universities, that " they turned their indomitable
energy to the pursuit of gain."‖   That there is an

* *Archiv*, vol. xx., p. 9.   † *Ibid.*, p. 10.
‡ *Economic Liberalism*, p. 64; Thorold Rogers, *History of
Agriculture and Prices*, vol. v., p. 145; Gardiner, *The Great Civil
War*, vol. iii., p. 11.
§ Troeltsch, *Soziallehren*, p. 780.
‖ *The Puritan in England, Holland, and America*, vol. ii., p. 401.

element of truth in this suggestion is undeniable; it would be absurd to contend that the exclusion of the members of any sect from public offices does not tend to drive them to earn their living by other means. That this was an important factor in the case of the Puritans is granted by Weber, Troeltsch, and Levy.* But it cannot be admitted to have been the only factor operating to connect Puritans with business and industrial careers. For one thing, it must be recollected that the Puritans exhibited precisely the same character in countries where they were the dominant majority, as in countries where they were the persecuted minority. The commercial faculties of Puritans seem to have developed more rather than less in America than in England, but it cannot be suggested that the Puritans in America were excluded from non-commercial careers. On the other hand, other sects have been the victims of persecution in other countries without developing any marked commercial genius. These considerations compel us to look further into the matter to see if there was not something internal in Puritanism which predisposed it to the encouragement and development of the industry and commerce of the modern world; in other words, if there was not something in Puritanism favourable to the growth of capitalism.

The answer to this inquiry will emerge if we recall to mind the peculiar Calvinist teaching of intramundane asceticism, which, as we have seen, reached its highest development in Puritanism. The most prominent duty of the Christian, according to this doctrine, the fulfilment of his calling and work—as distinguished from the

* *Archiv,* vol. xxi. p. 70; *Soziallehren,* p. 709; *Economic Liberalism,* p. 65.

old Catholic " works "—was extolled as the best means of glorifying God, and of proving one's own election. It is obvious that in a system of this kind, laziness and idleness would come to be regarded as most grievous offences. Thus it was that loss of time caused by luxury or idleness was the worst sin in the eyes of Puritans.* Baxter exhorts the faithful thus: " Keep up a high esteem of time, and be every day more careful that you lose none of your time than you are that you lose none of your gold and silver," and Matthew Henry, the author of the *Worth of the Soul,* says that " Those who are prodigal of their time despise their own souls." According to Weber, the maxim, " time is money," would have been acceptable to the Puritans, who, however, would have used it in the spiritual sense. Baxter held that constant activity in one's work led to diligence in prayer, and helped to ward off temptation; and he warns the man who neglects his work, even that he may indulge in religious meditation and contemplation, that he is sacrificing his greater duty to the pursuit of a less.† The same insistence on work is to be found in the Puritan attitude to the poor and to alms. We have already referred to this in the previous chapter, when we saw that the new attitude towards poor relief vigorously condemned all beggars and voluntary idlers. " The victory of Puritanism," according to Levy, " brought with it the apotheosis of work."‡

It is obvious that this insistence on the importance of work must have helped to stimulate production. " This conception of work," says Troeltsch, " gave a

---

* *Archiv,* vol. xxi., p. 77.   † *Archiv,* vol. xxi., p. 78.
    ‡ *Economic Liberalism,* p. 77; and see Cunningham, *The Moral Witness of the Church ;* and Troeltsch, *Soziallehren,* p. 711.

strong and systematic impulse to production."* We
have seen that one of the features of the *laissez faire*
school of economics, which we have described as being
the scientific exposition of the capitalist spirit, is the
stress it lays on production, compared with its comparative neglect of consumption. The desire for ever-
increasing production, which is a feature of the capitalistic spirit, was encouraged not only by the Puritan
conception of the fulfilment of the vocation, but also
by the other branch of the Puritan ascetic teaching—
namely, the observance of strict frugality and austerity.
The Puritan ideal of life was centred on the fulfilment of
one's vocation, and on the observance of the simplest
manner of living; it did not give any attention to the
lighter and more artistic side of life. Sports and games,
art, the drama, and beauty in personal adornment,
were all regarded with suspicion by the Puritans.†
There can be no doubt that the adoption of this ascetic
ideal tended to intensify the already strong attachment
of the Puritan to his trade or business. " It is indisputable," says Levy, " that the industrial capacity of
the believing Dissenter was strengthened by his abstin-
ence from games and sport. . . . The concentration on
exclusively economic activities, so noticeable in Dissent,
was increased by the antipathy shown to academic
learning, and generally to private devotion, to science, or
art, or similar occupations;"‡ and Mr. H. G. Wood says
that: " The capitalist class was largely created by men
who branded all careless consumption as a sin. The
Puritan conception of stewardship, and the Puritan

* *Soziallehren*, p. 955; and see Inge, *Outspoken Essays*, p. 256.
† Weber, *Archiv*, vol. xxi., pp. 92-6.
‡ *Economic Liberalism*, pp. 66-7.

condemnation of worldly living, will be found to have contributed more to the morals of capitalism than either the love of gain or any conscious adaptation of a class to their place in the productive process."* The Puritan conception of stewardship, to which Mr. Wood refers, was somewhat different from the old Catholic conception, and arose from the idea that property was a trust to be wisely invested and increased for the glorification of God. The parable of the talents was very popular among Puritans.†

It is obvious that the combination of these two ideals, which went to compose the ideal of intramundane asceticism, must have operated to encourage production and discourage consumption. This led to the accumulation of more and more capital, which, being considered a trust in the hands of its owner, must, in its turn, be invested and managed so as to bring the greatest possible return. This is a characteristically capitalist attitude, and it is undoubtedly at the same time a characteristically Puritan one. Puritan asceticism waged war against the improvident enjoyment of goods and unwise consumption, and also took away all the traditional hindrances which limited the desire for gain, which it not only legalized, but sanctified. Puritanism thus encouraged the formation of a characteristically capitalist point of view.‡

* *Property, Its Duties and Rights*, p. 154.

† Weber, *Archiv*, vol. xxi., p. 98.

‡ Weber, *Archiv*, vol. xxi., p. 101. " The Calvinistic insistence on the importance of the vocation," says Troeltsch, " had the result of giving an impetus to production, which was bound up at the same time with the ascetic view point; which condemned all luxury and unnecessary consumption. On this account Calvinism was favourable to the growth of urban capitalism. . . . The exhortation to continuous work, together with

All difficulties in the way of organizing industry on a capitalist basis were removed by the conception of the vocation; the worker fulfilled his vocation by ceaseless activity in his task, and the master by gaining the greatest profit possible.* The division of labour was approved, not for the reasons given by Thomas Aquinas and Luther, but because it tended to increase the quantitative and qualitative value of the work service —a utilitarian treatment, prophetic of Adam Smith.†

There are therefore many resemblances between the Puritan and the capitalist attitude towards economic life. The analogy, however, will not be complete unless we can point to some Puritan idea corresponding to the idea which we have seen to be the central thesis of the philosophy of *laissez faire*—namely, the harmony of private and public interests. The encouragement of increased production and of the incessant accumulation of capital could not produce the characteristically capitalist attitude so long as it was thought that the direction of individuals in their economic activities should rest with the state or with some other public authority. The complete relaxation of restraints on the pursuit of one's private gain and the absolute freedom of individual enterprise and ambition are essential components of what we have described as

---

the limitation of consumption and of luxury, effected a tendency to a growing formation of capital, which on its side, by the necessity of its further consumption in work, and not in enjoyment, again led the way to increased transactions; the command to work and the prohibition of luxury worked in their union as a compulsion to save, and the compulsion to save worked for the formation of capital." (*Soziallehren*, pp. 957 and 710.)

  * Weber, *Archiv*, vol. xx., p. 33; vol. xxi., pp. 106-7.
  † *Ibid.*, vol. xxi., p. 84.

capitalism. Can any corresponding ideas be found in Puritanism ?

We saw that the freedom of the individual was justified by the *laissez faire* school on the ground that it led to the greatest good of the greatest number, which was the *summum bonum* of a utilitarian age. But the *summum bonum* of Puritanism was the glorification of God and the assurance of the election of the justified, and Puritanism certainly taught, as we have seen, that this end could be attained only by the fulfilment of his vocation by each individual. But one's vocation could be fulfilled only by ceaseless activity and work. Therefore, the ceaseless activity and work of individuals was the way in which the *summum bonum* of Puritanism could be reached, just as it was the way in which the *summum bonum* of utilitarianism could be reached.

And here it is important to draw attention to the fact that the Puritan conception of society was not static like that of Lutheranism or Catholicism; every man was not only permitted, but bound, to change his occupation, if he saw that he would benefit by the change. It was taught that, when an opportunity of profit arose, it was a sign of God's providence, and that a good Christian should rise to the occasion. The parable of the talents was quoted to show that man must make the best use of his opportunities, and it was said that to wish to be poor was as unnatural as to wish to be sick.* Baxter's *Christian Directory* contains the following counsels: " It is no sin but a duty to labour not only for labour's sake, but for that honest increase and provision which is the end of our labour; and therefore to choose a gainful calling rather than another, so that we may be able to

* Weber, *Archiv*, vol. xxi., p. 86.

do good and relieve the poor;" and again: " If God
shows you a way in which you may lawfully get more
than in another way, if you refuse this and choose the
less gainful way, you cross one of the ends of your
calling, and you refuse to be God's steward."* Obviously,
if the course of action which promised the greatest gain
was one indicated by the Will of God, if, in other words,
the pursuit of gain was itself the subject of a vocation,
all restraints which hindered the individual from pursuing it must be regarded as wicked and unjustifiable.
Here we have a very powerful argument for *laissez
faire*.

The unrestricted freedom of the individual is thus
necessary in order that his vocation may be properly
fulfilled. We also find the idea expressed in Puritan
writings that the fulfilment of one's vocation is the best
service one can render to the community. Baxter says:
" It is action that God is most served and honoured by.
The public welfare or the good of the many is to be
valued above our own;"† and further: " You may cast
off all such excess of worldly cares or business as un-
necessarily hinder you in spiritual things. But you may
not cast off all bodily employment and mental labour in
which you may serve the common good. Every one as
a member of a Church or Commonwealth must employ
his parts to the utmost for the good of the Church and
the Commonwealth. To neglect this and say: ' I will
pray and meditate,' is as if your servant should refuse
your greatest work and tie him to some lesser easier
part."‡ " Restless activity in one's work," according

* Levy, *Economic Liberalism*, p. 60; *Property, Its Duties and
Rights*, p. 157.

† Weber, *Archiv*, vol. xxi., p. 75.   ‡ *Ibid.*, p. 78.

to Troeltsch, " as the best service for the religious community and the public welfare are the maxims and ideas
which stamp this group definitely."* This is getting
very near the *laissez faire* assumption of the harmony
of public and private interests. The fulfilment of one's
vocation is the best service that the individual can
render the community; but, in order that one may
fulfil one's vocation, all artificial restraints on private
enterprise must be abolished; therefore, in order that
the individual may render the best service to the community, all artificial restraints on private enterprise
must be abolished.

Before concluding our remarks on the importance of
the vocation idea in the formation of the capitalist
spirit, we must draw attention to another feature of
Calvinism, and particularly of Puritanism, that was
working in the same direction. The idea that prosperity and success were the tokens by which election
could be recognized had appeared once before—namely,
in Judaism. The Old Testament is permeated with the
conception of the chosen people, and the marks by
which the chosen people are distinguished from others
are their worldly glory and honour.† The analogy
between the standpoint of the Old Testament and that
of the modern capitalist is so striking that it is sometimes suggested that the growth of capitalism is the
result of the dispersal of the Jews through Europe.
That is the thesis of Sombart's great work, *The Jews*

* *Soziallehren*, p. 950; and see p. 575.
† " The Old Testament mentions scarcely any other reward
for the good, or any other punishment for the wicked, than the
gain or the loss of temporal goods. Wealth is considered as the
tangible proof of God's favour, as the reward of the pious man,
and poverty as a punishment." (Batault, *Le Problème juif*, p. 171.)

and Modern Capitalism. Nowadays, however, this thesis is generally rejected, in favour of that which we have endeavoured to present in the present chapter. As Troeltsch points out, there is a difference between the economic ideal of the Jew, who directs his attention primarily to trade and money-lending, and that of the capitalist, who directs it to manufacture and exploitation.* Moreover, some of the most characteristic developments of capitalism took place in countries where the presence of Jews was almost unknown—for example, Scotland in the eighteenth century.†

It must not be imagined for a moment that there is nothing in Sombart's suggestion. On the contrary, his contention would be quite correct if for the word " Jews " we substituted " Judaism." The influence of Old Testament ideas developed, not in communities where Jews were resident, but in communities where those ideas had been adopted by Christians. And the Christians by whom they were adopted were the Calvinists.

All Protestantism was inclined to rely very largely on the Old Testament. Luther based his ethical system on the Decalogue rather than on the Sermon on the Mount, and regarded Christ and the Apostles as merely the restaters and expositors of the Decalogue.‡ But it was the followers of Calvin, and especially the Puritans, who first elevated the Old Testament into a position of supreme importance. This elevation of the Old Testament was the inevitable result of seeking for a scriptural basis for everything, as there were many matters on which the New Testament was silent upon which much

* *Protestantism and Progress*, p. 142.
† Cunningham, *Christianity and Economic Science*, p. 69.
‡ Troeltsch, *Soziallehren*, p. 494.

could be found in the Old. " Calvinists," said Dr. Cunningham, " professed to find a scriptural basis for every detail of life in an organized Christian society, and they would have none other. This proved the fundamental weakness of their position; there are many matters of great importance, commercial, social, and political, about which the Christian scriptures give us no direct light at all. . . . On these questions (of ecclesiastical organization) and still more on economic matters of every kind, the New Testament fails to lay down any rules; and hence the Calvinists fall back on the will of God as declared in the Old Testament. During the Middle Ages the blanks in Gospel teaching had been filled up by reference to the stores of natural wisdom which was collected and formulated in the writings of Aristotle; natural reason was used, much as St. Paul had appealed to the natural conscience, to confirm and supplement the dicta of Christian morality. But the Calvinists discarded the great body of acute thought which had been raised on this double basis, and sought for direct guidance in the code which had been laid down for the ancient people of God. By so doing, they insensibly and unconsciously eliminated anything that was specifically Christian from their scheme of social morality, and fell back on the Old Testament and the Jewish standards of commercial dealings."*

What the Puritans found in the Old Testament fitted in precisely with the moral code which they were evolving out of their notions of predestination and the indestructibility of grace. " The duties of secular life

* *Christianity and Economic Science*, pp. 62-3; and see Campbell, *Puritan in Holland, England, and America*, vol. ii., p. 140; Weber, *Archiv*, vol. xxi., pp. 9, 33-4.

are more fully dealt with in the Book of Proverbs than in any other part of the Old Testament, and the teaching in that book on social and economic matters is entirely prudential in character; the vices of the self-indulgent and the sluggard are denounced, while diligence and thrift are commended. . . . There is nothing specifically Christian in the religious point of view which was thus adopted, either as regards the dignity of work, or the greed of gain."* The Old Testament idea of the reward of virtue in this world fitted in with the Puritan idea of the fulfilment of the vocation. Both notions supported the belief that a certain degree of human fulfilment could be reached on this earth. The chosen people proved themselves through the fulfilment of their earthly calling. The merchant sitting at his desk was contributing to the glorification of God.† The influence of the Old Testament is also seen in the constantly recurring chiliasm, which was a feature of English Dissent.‡ Characteristic, also, is the modern English respect for wealth and contempt for poverty: " Material prosperity in England bred a worship of wealth which has never been equalled, except possibly in old Judæa."§ An American, writing in 1886 of this feature of modern English life, remarked: "Much of the social power of wealth in England is due to a kind of sanctity which is attached to it, which comes, it is believed, from the Old Testament."‖ Emerson was much impressed by this

* Cunningham, *op. cit.*, p. 68.
† Schulze-Gavernitz, *op. cit.*, p. 29; Troeltsch, *Soziallehren*, p. 620.
‡ *Property, Its Duties and Rights*, p. 162.
§ Campbell, *The Puritan in Holland, England, and America* vol. ii., p. 402.
‖ *The Atlantic Monthly*, November, 1886, p. 620.

side of the English character. "There is no country," he wrote, "in which so absolute a homage is paid to wealth. . . . The Englishman has pure pride in his wealth, and esteems it a final certificate. . . . There is a mixture of religion in it. They are under the Jewish law, and read with sonorous emphasis that their days shall be long in the land, they shall have sons and daughters, flocks and herds, wine and oil. In exact proportion is the reproach of poverty. . . . The last term of insult is a 'beggar.' Sydney Smith said 'poverty is infamous in England.' "* It is interesting to note in this connection that the sumptuary regulations among early Calvinists made property the measure of distinction between the different classes. Troeltsch opines that this may have been the genesis of the plutocratic attitude of modern Dutch and American society.†

It is unnecessary for us to labour a point so generally admitted as the profound influence which the Old Testament exercised on Calvinism. This influence is recognized by Troeltsch,‡ and by Weber, who says that Puritanism is English Hebraism.§ Batault says that "Calvinism, in its ultimate analysis, is nothing else than an enlarged Judaism, freed from its narrow national

---

* *English Traits*, p. 86.

† *Soziallehren*, p. 731. Baxter thought that poverty was often a sign of spiritual evil. (Weber, *Archiv*, vol. xxi., p. 105.) The trading spirit in Scotland was first observed about 1700, at which time religious tracts and pamphlets became less common, and political and economic ones began to take their place. (Laing, *History of Scotland*, vol. iv., p. 291.) "Heretofore," according to Buckle, "persons were respected solely for their parentage; now they were also respected for their riches. . . . Instead of asking who a man's father was, the question became, How much had he got?" (*History of Civilization*, vol. ii., p. 311.)

‡ *Soziallehren*, pp. 638 and 652.

§ *Archiv*, vol. xxi., p. 90.

and ethnical limitations."* The influence of Judaism on Calvinism having been established, it is easy to see how we can reconcile Sombart's thesis with Weber's. Judaism has undoubtedly played a very large part in the development of modern capitalism, but it has played that part, not directly, through the residence of Jews in Christian communities, but indirectly, through its impressing itself upon the Calvinist mind.

The thesis that the modern capitalist spirit had its roots in Calvinism, and especially in Puritanism, has found practically unanimous support among all who have studied the matter. We shall conclude this chapter with some quotations from the writings of scholars of repute, which show how widely the thesis has been accepted in Germany, France, and England. Of course, the writer who has done most to lead it to its present position is Max Weber. Troeltsch, while differing from Weber on minor points, expresses his general agreement with him in the following passage: " When all is said and done, Calvinism remains the real nursing-father of the civic industrial capitalism of the middle classes. Self-devotion to work and gain, which constitutes the involuntary and unconscious asceticism of the modern man, is the child of a conscious ' intra-mundane ' asceticism of work and calling inspired by religious motives. The ' spirit of the calling,' which does not reach out beyond the world, but works in the world without ' creature worship '—that is, without love of the world—becomes the parent of a tireless systematic laboriousness, in which work is sought for work's sake, for the sake of the mortification of the

* *Le Problème juif*, p. 177, where quotations in the same sense are given from Taine, Guizot, Macaulay, Vermeil, etc.

flesh, in which the produce of the work serves, not to be consumed in enjoyment, but to the constant reproduction of the capital employed. Since the aggressively active ethic inspired by the doctrine of predestination urges the elect to the full development of his God-given powers, and offers him this as a sign by which he may assure himself of his election, work becomes rational and systematic. In breaking down the motive of ease and enjoyment, asceticism lays the foundations of the tyranny of work over men. And from the fact that the produce of this work is in no way an end in itself, but advances the general well-being, and that all return which goes beyond an adequate provision for the needs of life is felt to be merely a stimulus to the further employment and increase of it, there results the principle of the illimitability and infinitude of work. On the basis of this economic attitude there arose the early capitalism of the Huguenots, of Holland, England, and America; and even to the present day in America and Scotland, as well as among the English nonconformists, the higher capitalism is clearly seen to be closely connected with it. A similar development has taken place among the Pietistic groups, which were to a great extent allied to and influenced by Calvinism in this religious-ascetic idea; and also among the Baptist communities, which abandoned communion in favour of the Protestant ' ethic of the calling,' for they all, finding themselves excluded from public life, turned to economic activities, and, tabooing the aim of enjoyment, declared production for production's sake to be a commandment of religion. Weber has, in my opinion, completely proved his case."* Troeltsch also insists in several

* *Protestantism and Progress*, pp. 135-8.

passages that it is Calvinism that has given the modern
Anglo-Saxon world its peculiar complexion, and that it
is the only organized body of Christian opinion, except
Catholicism, which can be expected to survive in the new
conditions of society in the twentieth century. Outside
Christianity, there are, according to Troeltsch, many
conceivable social ideals, but, inside Christianity, there
are only two that can be adapted to modern life—namely,
those of Calvinism and Catholicism. The other forms
of Protestantism are too utopian to master the hard
facts of the battle for existence and of the clash of
interests under modern conditions. One of the distinguishing features of Calvinism, which enables it to
keep abreast of social developments, is that it renders
possible a conservative democracy, which is the great
political achievement of the Anglo-Saxon peoples.*
Other German scholars who agree with Weber's conclusions are Hermann Levy, who says: " To me there
is a close spiritual affinity between the economic ideas
of the seventeenth-century Puritans and the later
theories of individualism;"† and Schulze-Gavernitz,
who says that the Puritan conception of the fulfilment
of one's vocation " led in its practical consequences to
the separation of ethics from theology and metaphysics,
to a neglect of the sympathetic, as opposed to the
egoistic grounds of action. Out of this there arose
that atmosphere of practical materialism in which the
modern ' monied man ' lives."‡

The same view is generally accepted by French
students. Many years before Weber's essay appeared,
Baudrillart, the biographer of Bodin, called attention to

---

* *Soziallehren*, pp. 607, 609, 647-8, 674-5, 763-4, 769, 964.
† *Economic Liberalism*, p. 86.   ‡ *Op. cit.*, p. 12.

the strange paradox that Protestantism, which, from reliance on faith as apart from works, might have been expected to have exercised an enervating influence on industry, did, in fact, exercise the precisely opposite influence. " Protestantism has created industrial peoples. . . . That which appeared to be doomed to become purely mystical proved to be utilitarian even to excess."* " Calvinism," according to E. Vermeil, " has seized the bond between moral and economic progress. Is it not favouring capitalism to preach work, and, at the same time, to condemn luxury ? Calvinism has glorified work as the realization of the Divine purpose. It is by that that it has favoured the economic evolution of the modern world."†   Batault remarks that Weber's thesis is now disputed by nobody.‡

English scholarship is also unanimous on this matter. Nearly a hundred years ago, Robert Southey put the following words into the mouth of Sir Thomas More in his famous dialogue: " In some things, and those essential ones, the Protestants brought back a corrupted faith to its primitive purity. But it is not less certain that the Reformation has, in its consequences, lowered the standard of devotion, lessened the influence of religion, not among the poor and ignorant alone, but among the classes; and prepared the way for the uncontrolled dominion of that worldly spirit which it is the tendency of the commercial spirit to produce and foster."§   Many years later, Morris and Bax wrote: " The mystical individualist ethics of Christianity, which had for its supreme end another world and

* *Jean Bodin et son Temps*, p. 43.
† *Études sur la Réforme*, p. 905.
‡ *Op. cit.*, p. 187.   § *Sir Thomas More*, p. 158.

spiritual salvation therein, has been transformed into an individualist ethic, having for its supreme end, tacitly, if not avowedly, the material salvation of the individual in the commercial battle of this world. This is illustrated by the predominance among the commercial classes of a debased Calvinistic theology, termed Evangelicalism, which is the only form of religion these classes can understand—the poetico-mystical element in the earlier Christianity being eliminated therefrom, and the ' natural laws ' of profit and loss, and the devil take the hindmost, which dominate this carnal world, being as nearly as possible reproduced into the spiritual world of its conception."* The late Dr. Cunningham was of opinion that it was " not necessary to labour a point " so widely admitted as the fact that " Calvinism is a form of Christianity which gave its sanction to the free existence of the commercial spirit and to the capitalist organization of industry."† Mr. H. G. Wood says: " It would be scarcely fair to criticize the Puritan outlook, because it failed to anticipate the social evils of the industrial revolution, although it would deserve censure if by its concentration on individual duty it rendered man blind to the necessity of common action, and perhaps a little callous towards the evils in question. Undoubtedly later Puritanism had this latter effect, although other evils of eighteenth-century life also co-operated to produce it. Many good men of the Puritan stock were, and perhaps are to-day, attached obstinately to the principle of *laissez faire*, because a rooted trust in individual responsibility and self-help is part of their religious inheritance. . . . In this, Puritanism displays

---

* *Socialism, Its Growth and Outline*, p. 10.
† *Christianity and Economic Science*, pp. 69-70.

the defects of its qualities. . . . The close connection between the Puritan ethic of prudence and the spirit of capital is undeniable."*

On the whole, it is difficult to resist the conclusion that the capitalist spirit had a Calvinistic foundation. Capitalism is therefore one of the economic products of the Reformation; let us now discuss its other great product, socialism.

* *Property, Its Duties and Rights*, pp. 151 and 157; and see Ashley, *The Economic Organization of England*, p. 158; Tawney, *Acquisitive Society*, pp. 10-11; Inge, *Outspoken Essays*, p. 256; Palgrave, *Dictionary of Political Economy*, art. " Christianity and Economics." Conrad Noel, *Socialism and Church History*, p. 198. Preserved Smith says that Weber's essay has made " Capitalism and Calvinism " one of the watchwords of contemporary thought. (*The Age of the Reformation*, p. 728.)

CHAPTER III

Protestantism and Socialism

AS we began the last chapter with a definition of what we meant by capitalism, we must begin this with a definition of what we mean by socialism—the other great school of economic thought that prevails at the present day. Of course, the term " socialism " is used to cover many different kinds of economic organization, ranging from communism on the one hand to the mere state supervision of industrial conditions on the other; but, with all its vagueness and loose usage, the term does convey a certain more or less definite meaning. We are not going through all the definitions of the word " socialism " which have been given by those who have dealt with the subject, but shall content ourselves with indicating what the common use of the term implies.

The first and most obvious characteristic of socialism is that it stands opposed to the unrestrained individualism which we indicated in the last chapter as characteristic of capitalism. Far from assenting to Adam Smith's assumption that the interests of the community are best served by each individual's pursuing his own private interest as energetically as he can, socialists believe that the practical application of this maxim has been productive of untold hardship and poverty to the working classes, and of widespread misery to society. They are impressed—and justly impressed—by the breakdown of unregulated individualism in the economic sphere, which they suggest—and suggest correctly—has led to plutocracy on the one hand, and to pauperism on the other; and they consequently insist on the necessity for the reintroduction of some principle of justice into the domain of distribution, and into economic life in general. As to what this principle should be, there was no general agreement among the early socialists: the Saint - Simonians would have divided the economic product according to capacity and work; the Fourierists according to capital, labour, and ability; the Communists according to no principle but that of equality; and Louis Blanc according to the needs of the consumer.* But, with the passage of time, and the gradual retreat of utopian, and the advance of scientific socialism, the principle of securing to the worker the enjoyment of the total product of his labour has tended to become the main principle of socialist justice. Rae's definition, given in 1884, is probably accurate to-day: " Socialism is a theory of the state's action, founded on a theory of the labourer's right—at bottom a demand for social justice—that every man shall possess the whole produce of his labour."†

This definition draws attention to a second point—namely, that socialism is " a theory of the state's action." In other words, the administration of the new principle of justice, which is to take the place of un-restrained competition in social life, is to be under the guidance and direction of the state. The whole basis of socialism is the omnipotence and omniscience of the state, and the relative unimportance of the life of the

* Sudre, *Histoire du Communisme*, p. 451.
† *Contemporary Socialism*, p. 13.

individual compared with that of the society in which
he lives. The mediæval view was that society was
made for man, but the socialist view is that man was
made for society, and that all his activities must be
directed so as to ensure that they will effect the greatest
possible benefit to the community. One corollary of
this principle is that the question of the distribution of
the economic product is a public and not a private
affair, and that it must consequently be regulated by
the public authorities.

Obviously, this is a very fundamental and far-reaching suggestion and, when pushed to its logical conclusion,
is incompatible with the existence of any private rights.
That is why the word " socialism " has come to be
associated so very generally with the attack on property,
which it certainly implies. Every school of socialism
has demanded the abolition of existing property rights
to a greater or less degree, and the demand for the
abrogation of other private rights—marital, parental,
etc.—is only another application of the same principle.
Sometimes the attack has been on every species of property, sometimes only on property used for productive
purposes, and sometimes only on property in land; but
the ultimate attack on all private rights of every kind is
always latent in socialism, even though it may not be
claimed to its fullest extent.

Having made clear what we mean by socialism, we
pass on to show the connection which, we suggest, existed
between it and the teaching of the Reformation. This
connection was of two kinds: in the first place, socialism
was the reaction against the unregulated individualism,
manifesting itself as capitalism, which we have shown to
have been based upon reformed teaching; and, in the

second place, socialism found arguments and encourage-
ments in certain distinctive doctrines of the Reformation.
We shall deal with these two kinds of connection
separately: first, dealing with socialism, in so far as it
was a reaction against capitalism; and, secondly, dealing
with it in so far as it was the logical outcome of certain
doctrines of the Reformation.

It may be suggested that socialism, in so far as it
represents a reaction against capitalism, cannot be
shown to be a result of the Reformation. It is true
that the connection is indirect, but it is none the less
real on that account. If a certain body of teaching on
religious matters produces a certain theory of society,
which errs by laying too much importance on certain
elements of social life, it cannot escape the responsibility
of being the indirect cause of all the other theories of
society which have their origin in the reaction against
the first. It is true that the reaction against an error
probably goes too far in the opposite direction, and
indeed, socialism does so; but this is merely to say that
error breeds error, and that it is of the very essence of
heresy to lead to the most widely divergent results.*
The later sects which arose among Protestants frequently
arose as a protest against the errors of previous ones, and
they almost invariably erred in the opposite direction;
but nobody would suggest that the original heresy was
not responsible for all its children, however little they
resembled each other; and so, similarly, the Reformation

* " Il y a une loi de l'esprit humain, une opposition naturelle
des génies et des opinions, qui veut que toute doctrine extrême
soit combattue par la doctrine diamétralement contraire, jusqu'à
ce que la vérité et la raison, ou tout au moins une modération et
une sagesse relatives, les aient écartées l'une et l'autre." (Franck,
Réformateurs et Publicistes, vol. i., p. 338.)

must be held responsible for all the social errors as well as for the religious errors to which it gave birth.

In view of the extent to which unrestrained capitalism had been allowed to grow, it was inevitable, in the nature of things, that some reaction would be provoked. The gross inequalities of fortune arising out of the play of unrestrained individualism; the spectacle of the greatest benefits from new inventions and industries being reaped by a favoured few, while the unfortunate many sank into a condition of propertyless dependence; and the manifest failure of gigantic advances in production to secure any just system of distribution, inevitably led social reformers, publicists, and all who had suffered injury from the existing regime to devise remedies and propose expedients for the reform of society. These suggestions frequently went to the length of attacking uses apart from abuses. Thus the very institutions of property and of the existence of an employing class came to be questioned, regardless of the fact that what was evil was not these institutions, but the abuses of which they were the occasion.*

The close connection between the excesses of capitalism and the appearance of socialist reaction is shown by the fact that the birth of modern socialism may be traced to the place and time at which individualism had reached its worst excesses—namely, the England of the early nineteenth century. This is well put by Beer in his *History of British Socialism:* " The reign of George IV. marks the rise of Liberalism and the birth of the modern Labour movement, political and socialistic. This decade

---

* Balmez, *op. cit.,* p. 227; and see Tawney, *op. cit.,* p. 56, where it is pointed out that the rise of capitalism was itself a reaction against the undue interference of governments.

saw the repeal of the Navigation Act, of the Combination Laws, of the Corporation and Test Acts; it witnessed the destruction of the last remnants of the yeomanry and the bulk of the handloom weavers; in it occurred a short but phenomenal spell of manufacturing and commercial prosperity, accompanied by the biggest and hardest fought strikes which the country had until then experienced; after which one of the severest commercial crises overtook the nation, and the temper of agrarian and industrial labour became restive and rebellious. ' King Ludd ' reappeared in the manufacturing centres, and ' Captain Swing ' devastated the counties by fire. Capitalism appeared to be on its trial. Thinking people began to read Adam Smith again; to pore over Ricardo with a critical eye; and even Owen, the visionary, found favour with some intellectuals. An era of economic criticism and cooperative experiment was ushered in, which laid the foundation of modern socialism, in the midst of a gloomy atmosphere, and full of forebodings of the impending bankruptcy of capitalism. Socialism, at its birth, imbibed the dogma that industrialism meant short spells of prosperity, followed by chronic crises, pauperization of the masses, and the sudden advent of the social revolution."* "We may regard socialism," according to Professor Foxwell, "as a protest against the extravagances of the individualistic movement of the Renaissance and the Reformation. . . . As a reaction against the anarchy of individualism, socialism naturally developed in proportion to the exaggerations of the fashionable philosophy; and when this found its *reductio ad absurdum* in the extreme *laissez faire* of the

* Vol. i., p. 182.

' New School ' of economists, about the early forties, the tide of socialist influence reached its first high-water mark.   If this is a true view of the nature of the socialist movement, it is not surprising that it should have originated in England; and even those to whom socialism is the gospel of the future have no ground for national self-glorification on this account.   It is only natural that the reaction against the power of modern capital, and the mischief incidental to licence and absence of control, should begin in the country where that power first made itself felt, where its licence was most unbounded, and where it attained the most striking proportions."*   The growing discontent with the capitalist system tended to throw economic thinkers into two schools: on the one hand, the cynics and pessimists, who despaired of ever improving the condition of society, and, on the other hand, the utopians, who hoped for social regeneration through some socialistic scheme. The chief representative of the former school was Malthus, and of the latter, Godwin.†

The progress of socialistic ideas was aided by the weakness of the foundations of the system they attacked. Extreme individualism, based on the right of private judgment, had deprived society of a great part of its organic solidarity and of its power of resistance to attack, and had left it no principle to oppose to socialists but that of the social value of enlightened self-interest,

* Introduction to English translation of Menger's *Right to Whole Produce of Labour*, p. xxv.
† Leslie Stephen, *English Thought in the Eighteenth Century*, vol. ii., p. 327.   Ingram says: " Alongside of the evils of the new industrial system, socialism appeared as the alike inevitable and indispensable expression of the protest of the working classes and the aspiration after a better order of things." (*Op. cit.*, p. 112.)

which had been pretty thoroughly exploded by experience. Any critic of the existing order had an easy task; abuse had been piled on abuse; the capitalist system had become so foul that its perfections were even more objectionable than its defects; and the very successes of socialistic propaganda show how vulnerable must have been the institutions which it attacked.* John Stuart Mill drew attention to the fact that the defenders of private property in his day were standing for a system, which was so full of abuses that it stank in the nostrils of many decent men, who had never had an opportunity of experiencing a system of private property, properly administered. Mill says: " If we had to choose between private property, as it is now, and communism, we might elect for the latter in spite of its difficulties. But it is a rule of good criticism to compare the best form of one thing with the best form of its rival; and we should take private property, not as it is, but as it might be."†

Thus the progress of socialistic ideas was aided at every point by the excesses of capitalist individualism. Indeed, some of the most characteristic doctrines of the classical economists were seized on by socialists, and shown to be two-edged swords. Bentham, for example, was violently anti-communistic, but his insistence upon the greatest happiness of the greatest number was eagerly seized on by socialists, who also derived considerable inspiration from Ricardo's theory of value.‡ Indeed, it is interesting to note in passing that the socialist theory that labour is the source of all value can be traced back not only to Ricardo, but to the

* Nicolas, *op. cit.*, p. 419; Batault, *op. cit.*, p. 201.
† Bonar, *Philosophy and Political Economy*, pp. 254-5.
‡ Beer, *op. cit.*, vol. i., pp. 104-5, 189.

English Puritans of the seventeenth century, and even to Luther.*

Socialism, having come into existence as a protest and reaction against excessive capitalism, was coloured by some of the characteristics of the system it attacked. Unlike the communism of the Middle Ages, which was self-abnegatory and world-denying, modern scientific socialism has imbibed much of the avaricious, self-seeking spirit of the capitalist society which it aimed at displacing. " That the new philosophy of right," says Professor Foxwell, " should contain fundamental inconsistencies is what we might expect if we consider its historical development. On the one hand, like the crude political economy which it attacked, it was founded upon the highly individualistic theory of natural right; while, on the other, it was a reaction against unprecedented individual licence, in favour of collectivist organization for the general welfare. The earlier philosophies, like those of Owen and Thompson, were more inclined to protest against self-interest and competition, and to inculcate a spirit of altruism and a system of communism. The Marxian socialists have appealed very frankly to the most primitive of the individualistic instincts, and have laid more stress on the confiscation of the existing forms of property than on the nature of the new system of distribution."†

Modern socialism thus drew its materialistic character from the individualism against which it was the reaction. It made its appearance in a materialistic age, in which concern for the body took precedence of concern for the

* Levy, *Economic Liberalism*, p. 77; Erhardt, *op. cit.*, p. 688; and see some interesting remarks by Beer, *op. cit.*, vol. i., p. 189.
† *Op. cit.*, pp. xix-xx.

soul and the mind, and in which progress was thought of in terms of material comfort. " Socialism has always worked within the framework of materialistic thought. It is a reaction against overstrained individualism in the same framework, and, because it was a reaction, its advocates believed themselves to be idealists. . . . The difference between the *laissez faire* school and the socialists is one of method, not of aim; but it is the aim that makes the ideal, and the aim of both was, and is, comfort. The one stressed the production, the other the diffusion of wealth; but it was wealth all the time. Of course, this was to lead to other things, but comfort came first. It was to be the foundation, and the appeal has always been to appetite."* The fact that socialism arose in an age of high industrial development, and that it was stimulated largely by industrial grievances, accounts for the fact that, in attempting to introduce some equitable principle into economic distribution, it sought rather to adapt its ethical principle to the necessities of the economic situation rather than the opposite.† The absolute rights of labour which lie at the foundation of the socialist creed are almost as uncompromising and ruthless as the absolute rights of property which lie at the foundation of the capitalist creed.‡

Modern socialism, therefore, received a great impetus from the excessive individualism against which it was largely meant as a protest. Not only did the excessive individualism of the classical economists provide the opportunity for the development of socialist ideas; it also provided socialism with some useful dialectical

---

* This quotation is taken from an excellent article in the *Times Literary Supplement*, December 15, 1921.

† Batault, *op. cit.*, p. 188.   ‡ Tawney, *op. cit.*, p. 31.

weapons out of its own armoury, and imparted to it many of its own most characteristic traits. It is unquestionable that the modern socialist movement was largely created by *laissez faire* capitalism; and as the latter, as has been demonstrated, was one of the products of the Reformation, the former can also be traced, though less directly, to the same source. That is one of the links which we suggest connects socialism with the Reformation; the others, to which we now pass, were more direct, being certain positive doctrines preached by the reformers, which were attended—unintentionally, it is true—by socialistic consequences.

We may, perhaps, in the first place, draw attention to the close connection which has always existed between heretical and communist ideas. From the very first century of its existence the Church has had to fight against and condemn heretics and sectaries who were infected with communistic ideas, and innumerable heresies, which at first appeared purely religious, tended to provoke a spirit of communism amongst some of their adherents. As Kautsky says: " If the struggle to establish a communistic order of society necessarily conduced to heresy, so, on the other hand, the struggle with the Church favoured the growth of communistic ideas."*

One reason why communistic ideas almost invariably accompany outbreaks of heresy is that, when authority in one sphere is questioned, it will be questioned in every other sphere as well. Once the spiritual authority of

* *Communism in Central Europe*, p. 9. On the intimate connection between pre-Reformation heresy and communism, see Nicolas, *op. cit.*, pp. 300 *et seq.*, and Rambaud, *Histoire des Doctrines économiques*, pp. 612-3.

the Church is assailed, there is nothing to prevent assaults on the political authority of the state, and on the economic authority of the owner of property. The more radical and deep-seated the attack on the spiritual authority, the more far-reaching will its consequences be on other departments of life; and when, as in the case of the mediæval Church, every branch of secular life is deeply rooted in an ecclesiastical foundation, the consequences of heresy are bound to be momentous in the extreme.* The founders of the revolt against authority may be animated by purely religious motives, and may regard the social programme of their followers with extreme disfavour; but they are, nevertheless, responsible for opening the flood-gates through which a sea of revolution and anarchy may enter society. " One cannot," said Louis Blanc, " stop thought once it has revolted and has begun to march. The claim for the liberty of the Christian led irresistibly to the claim for the liberty of the whole man. Luther, whether he wished it or not, led straight to Münzer. The sixteenth century was the century of intelligence in revolt; it prepared, beginning with the Church, the ruin of every ancient power: that is what characterizes it."†

If it is true generally that heretical ideas tend to favour the growth of communism, it is particularly true of the Reformation, which placed the private judgment of the individual in the forefront of its programme.

* " The demolition of the authority of the Roman Church," says Troeltsch, " destroyed the prototypal form of the conception of life as dominated by authority." (*Protestantism and Progress*, p. 150; Batault, *Le Problème juif*, p. 175; and Roscher, *Geschichte der Nationalökonomik in Deutschland*, pp. 80, 90.)

† Quoted in Nicolas, *op. cit.*, p. 144.

Luther, who proclaimed the right of every person to interpret the scriptures in his own way, could scarcely complain if some of his followers found sentiments in them of which he did not himself approve. Münzer applied his private judgment to the scriptures, and apparently what he found in them was that the titles of the nobility and landed proprietors of his day were a gross usurpation; and he found quite a number of discontented peasants who were willing to agree with him in this view and to put right this wrong, by force if necessary. Luther could not logically resist this claim, which rested on the application of his own principle; and he was forced to take refuge in a maze of inconsistency, in which he not only denied to others the right of private judgment which he had claimed for himself, but contradicted some of his earlier and more indiscreet utterances on the wickedness of the lords and the wrongs of the poor.*

We drew attention earlier in this essay to the fact that the Reformation acted as an encouragement to the sects already in existence, which had been kept in check by the power of the undivided Church. Many of these heretics had communistic leanings. There is a clear line of descent to be traced between the communism preached by the Hussites and the other mediæval communists and that professed by the Anabaptists.† In

* Nicolas, pp. 140-1; Erhardt, *Theologische Studien und Kritiken*, 1880, p. 698; Baudrillart, *Jean Bodin et son Temps*, pp. 30-31; Schmoller, *op. cit.*, pp. 692, 694; Dide, *J. J. Rousseau, le Protestantisme et la Révolution française*. Schapiro says that " Münzer took up the peasants' cause with the idea of bettering, not their condition, but their souls. At bottom he was the *reductio ad absurdum* of a Luther." (*Op. cit.*, p. 72.)

† Troeltsch, *Soziallehren*, p. 409; Nicolas, *op. cit.*, pp. 370-2.

both cases the original leaders of the religious heresy had no intention of opening the door to a social revolution, but in both cases they were unable to prevent the consequences of their own actions. " Wycliffe's attitude towards the peasants' revolt," says Beer, " was similar to, though less violent than, that of Luther towards the German *Bauernkrieg;* and John Hus would, in all probability, have taken up the same attitude towards the Taborite wars in Bohemia, had he lived to witness them. The chief leaders of the Reformation brought their reforming zeal to bear upon ecclesiastical and national affairs, and left social grievances to be removed by the operation of ethical endeavour. The times were, however, out of joint, and the Reformation movement was, in all these countries, accompanied by social upheavals. The three reformers had their revolutionary counterparts in John Ball, Andrew Prokop, and Thomas Münzer, respectively, who, as priests, started from the same theological premises as the reformers, but were launched on their revolutionary careers by their democratic conception of mediæval communism. Legend or tradition makes Ball a disciple of Wycliffe, Münzer a disciple of Luther, while Prokop was actually a professed adherent of Hus."*

In view of the connection which has always existed between heretical and communist ideas, it is interesting to notice that the first genuinely communist movement that England experienced after the Reformation occurred under the Commonwealth, when the Church principle was at its lowest and the independent principle at its height. Kett's rebellion was in no sense a communist manifestation, being merely fought against enclo-

* *Op. cit.,* vol. i., p. 26.

sures;* the Anabaptists who had come to England in
the early seventeenth century were not of the communist
variety;† and the Levellers were purely political in their
aims, which did not include any social equalitarianism.‡
But the Diggers, who appeared in 1649, presented all
the features of a true communist movement, and it is
probable that some of the published utterances of their
leader, Winstanley, were not without their influence on
Bellers, who, in his turn, influenced Owen.§

The heretical communism which infected the followers
of the reformers, like that which had infected the
mediæval sects, was something quite different from the
idealist communism of the early Church at Jerusalem,
and from the communism aimed at as a counsel of
perfection by the monks of the Church. The one was
confiscatory and compulsory, and designed for immediate
operation; whereas the other was charitable, voluntary,
and was clearly recognized as impossible of universal
attainment. The communism of Sir Thomas More's
Utopia was of the latter variety; and it is altogether
unfair and incorrect to include More amongst the communists of the Reformation. Sir Thomas More was

* Russell, *Kett's Rebellion ;* Gooch, *English Democratic Ideas,*
pp. 34 *et seq.*

† Gooch, *op. cit.,* p. 74.   On the comprehensiveness of the term
" Anabaptism," which included all sorts of different movements,
see Stern, *Die Sozialisten der Reformationszeit,* pp. 23-4.

‡ Gooch, *op. cit.,* pp. 139-41, 153, 208; Gardiner, *History of
the Commonwealth,* vol. i., pp. 47-9.

§ On this very interesting and not widely known movement,
see Berens, *The Digger Movement ;* Troeltsch, *Soziallehren,* pp.
821-4; Beer, *op. cit.,* vol. i., pp. 60 *et seq.*; Gooch, *op. cit.,* pp. 214-25;
the same author's *Political Thought from Bacon to Halifax,* pp.
122-32; Gardiner, *History of the Commonwealth,* vol. ii., pp. 5-6;
Bernstein, *Geschichte des Sozialismus,* I., vol. ii., p. 507; Levy,
Economic Liberalism, p. 77.

under no illusions about the practicability of his own perfect society; he realized the limits set to human perfectibility; and he would have been the first to condemn as " utopian "—in the modern sense—any suggestion to translate his ideals into realities.*

Heretical communism had far more analogy with the modern socialist movement than with early Christian communism. " Early Christian communism," according to Kautsky, " was unpolitical and passive. Proletarian communism, on the contrary, ever since the Middle Ages, has necessarily been political and rebellious where circumstances were favourable."† The communism of the Reformation is superficially distinguished from the socialistic movement of to-day, inasmuch as it aimed at the communization of the economic product, whereas modern socialism aims at the communization of the means of production.‡ But this distinction is only on the surface, and is simply the reflection of the economic conditions of the ages in which the two movements appeared; and it must not blind us to the essential similarities between the communism of the Reformation and modern socialism, both of which preach confiscation of existing rights, and the right of the community to dictate as regards the economic life of the individual. Wiskemann says that " Thomas Münzer, Karlstadt, and

---

* This is the view taken by Baudrillart, *Jean Bodin et son Temps*, p. 25; by Beer, *History of British Socialism*, vol. i., p. 32; by Roscher, *Geschichte*, p. 42; by Cathrein, *Socialism, Its Theoretical Basis and Practical Application*, p. 22; by Rambaud, *Histoire des Doctrines économiques*, p. 619; and by Franck, *Réformateurs et Publicistes*, vol. i., p. 361.

† *Communism in Central Europe*, p. 28.

‡ Bax, *Rise and Fall of the Anabaptists*, Preface and vol. iii., p. 389.

all the other leaders of the Anabaptists and the Swiss Libertines were the forerunners of the English Levellers, of the present-day communists, and of all the greater or lesser communistic societies erected since that time."*

The influence of the sixteenth-century communists was greatly strengthened, and their programme given an appearance of practicability, by the spectacle of the confiscation of the monastic lands. No attack on any institution can be strictly localized, but every assault tends to spread in a way totally unforeseen by its originators. It is the inevitable consequence of treating with contempt any particular species of property that all other species will be treated with similar contempt when the temptation and opportunity arise. It is impossible to abrogate another person's title to his property without opening the way to an attack upon one's own title.

Very frequently the violation of a right precedes its denial; and theories of justification are often invented to legitimize accomplished facts. People often make a theory of justification to suit their own case. This happened very widely at the time of the Reformation; the Church lands were confiscated from motives of rapacity, and then specious theories of justification were invented to confirm the new possessors in their titles. Thus Melancthon asserted that property was a natural right; but he was obliged to qualify his opinion in order to justify the Protestant princes in confiscating the wealth of the monasteries; and he proposed the rather far-reaching doctrine that those who made bad use of

---

* *Darstellung der in Deutschland zur Zeit der Reformation herrschenden nationalökonomischen Ansichten*, p. 142; and see Stern, *Die Sozialisten der Reformationszeit*, p. 88.

their property might be deprived of it by the political authorities.*   The danger inherent in such theories is similar to that inherent in private judgment in matters of faith; it is difficult to prevent others from using one's own weapons against oneself; and the danger is especially great when the dispossessors of the original owners do not see eye to eye with each other as to the distribution of the spoils.   " The return to primitive Christianity," says Kautsky, " the restoration of ' the pure word of God,' which the papal Church had falsified and interpreted in a sense opposed to the true one—these were the objects striven for by all parties and classes who were enemies to the papacy.   It must be confessed that each of these parties construed ' the pure word of God ' differently, and in a manner consonant with its own interests.   Only on one point were they unanimous— the despoliation of the Church."†   But as soon as the despoliation was successfully accomplished, serious differences of opinion arose as to how the proceeds were to be divided.   The poor naturally thought that they were entitled to the land that had originally been devoted to their succour, but, in fact, both in Germany and England, the nobles succeeded in appropriating the bulk of the confiscated property.‡   The point is that the security of the titles of the new owners of the ecclesiastical property must have been seriously diminished by the method by which their possessions had been obtained, and that the poor were naturally little inclined to respect property which had been obtained through the denial of the proprietary rights of other persons. The spectacle of the violent transfer of large quantities

* Dunning, *History of Political Thought*, vol. ii., p. 18.
† *Op. cit.*, p. 10.   ‡ *Ibid.*, p. 128.

of property, without any regard to the rights of its owners, must have had the effect of greatly lowering the respect for proprietary rights generally, and of opening the door to further attacks from communists and revolutionaries of all kinds.*

In this respect—as, indeed, in many others—the French Revolution presents a striking analogy to the Reformation. In both cases, attacks on ecclesiastical property were followed by attacks on all property. The French Revolution was in no sense a communist movement, and the absolute rights of property were strongly proclaimed and insisted on by the leaders. The communistic ideas of Mably and Morelly were not shared by the promoters of the Revolution, who, indeed, were violently opposed to any attack on property in general.† But, as in the case of the Reformation, if the right of property was not denied, it was violated. " The Revolution," according to Sudre, " violated great principles which it did not deny."‡ The suppression of the feudal rights and the confiscation of the goods of the clergy were not intended to effect a renovation of society or a destruction of property; it was in view of the affranchisement of free individual property that the feudal rights were suppressed; and it was simply with the wish to aid the state and to inaugurate a new system of relations

* Villeneuve Bargemont, *op. cit.*, vol. i., p. 305; Nicolas, *op. cit.*, p. 195; Gooch, *English Democratic Ideas in the Seventeenth Century*, p. 206. That there is no essential difference between ecclesiastical and other confiscations is pointed out in Matthew Arnold's *Irish Essays*, pp. 25-6.

† *Cambridge Modern History*, vol. viii., p. 33. " There are passages in Rousseau which imply that much is amiss in the existing distribution of wealth; but nowhere does he suggest that it would be either possible or desirable to introduce communism."

‡ *Histoire du Communisme*, p. 250.

with the Church that the goods of the clergy were confiscated. The sacredness of the property of individuals was, in principle, as much respected by the republic as by the old monarchy. The property of the *émigrés* was confiscated only because they had been deemed guilty of a political offence; while the requisitions and other military measures of the revolutionaries were analogous to the seizure of stores and the destruction of houses by an army in wartime, and were in no sense dictated by communist principles.*

These confiscations, however, were a violation of proprietary rights, and, as in the case of the confiscations at the time of the Reformation, the justification was soon forthcoming. The doctrine which was put forward was that property is a creation of the state, and can be abrogated by its creator—a doctrine which had been foreshadowed by Montesquieu,† and clearly enunciated by Voltaire,‡ and which was to be pushed to its logical conclusion by more advanced thinkers in later years.§ Thus, although the effect of the Revolution was to increase the number of landed proprietors in France, and greatly to increase the legal powers of the owners of property, it really sapped the foundation of the very right itself. The purely civil origin of proprietary rights

* *Cambridge Modern History*, vol. viii., p. 34; Bonar, *Philosophy and Political Economy*, p. 144; Bax, *The Last Episode of the French Revolution*, p. 251; Morris and Bax, *Socialism, Its Growth and Outline*, p. 150; Rambaud, *Histoire des Doctrines économiques*, pp. 636.

† *Esprit des Lois*, Book XXVI., chap. xv.

‡ *Dictionnaire philosophique*, vol. ii., p. 432.

§ The complete subordination of the rights of individual properties to the community was a necessary implication of Rousseau's teaching on the social contract. (Baudrillart, *Études de Philosophie morale*, vol. i., p. 94.)

was illustrated by the wide range of limitations in favour of the state created by revolutionary legislation, and by the simultaneous interference with the free right of testamentary disposition.*

The confiscations of the revolutionary period had the effect of weakening the respect accorded to proprietary rights in general, and of making easier the task of the communists in later years. Bax says that: " The nationalization, with a view to subsequent division, of the property of the clergy and emigrant nobles, had familiarized the people's minds generally with the idea of confiscation, and had correspondingly weakened the sentiment of the absoluteness of property as such."†

Louis Blanc admitted that the advance of communism had been facilitated by the confiscations of the Revolu- tion: " In submitting to discussion the legitimacy of ecclesiastical property, the Assembly, without knowing it, invited the people to discuss the inviolability of lay property; they opened abysses of which they did not perceive the depth. The result was thus twofold and contradictory in appearance; many proprietors were enriched; but the rights of private property were pro- foundly shaken."‡ The communists of 1848 simply applied the same principle of social inutility to the *nouveaux riches* of the Revolution that the revolutionaries

* Sagnac, *La Législation civile*, pp. 189, 191, 197, 226; Jouffroy, *Les Principes de la Révolution française* in Migne, *Encycl. Théol.*, Series II., vol. xix., p. 1302. It is worth remarking in passing that the progress of the Revolution was aided by the fact that the Church in France had been weakened by its struggle with Jan- senism, a heresy of a distinctly Calvinistic tone. On this see Buckle, *History of Civilization*, vol. ii., pp. 776, 849-50; *Catholic Encyclopædia*, art. " Jansenism."

† *The Last Episode of the French Revolution*, p. 254.

‡ *Histoire de la Révolution française*, vol. iii., p. 23.

had applied to the clergy; Jacobinism, Babœufism, the Socialism of 1830, and the Communism of 1848 were all simply different applications of the same principle.*

We refer to the French Revolution only because it provides an interesting parallel to the Reformation in one respect. In both cases the confiscation of ecclesiastical property weakened the respect with which property in general was regarded, and thus made the way easier for the progress of communist ideas. Another way in which the Reformation weakened the respect for property was by the diminution of private charity which followed it, owing to the insistence on the doctrine of justification by faith alone. We have already referred to this matter, and only desire now to draw attention to the fact that differences between rich and poor are much more tolerable, and are, indeed, frequently a source of good instead of evil, when charity is widely practised by the owners of property. Throughout the Middle Ages the duties of owners of property in respect of alms were very stringent and far-reaching; but, after the Reformation, a different conception of the duties of the rich towards the poor arose, and there can be little doubt that the gradually increasing selfishness of proprietors operated to encourage attacks on property in general, and to foment communistic and confiscatory movements.† The confiscation of Church property also had this effect, because the Church estates were always regarded as the most important source of charity for the poor, and these confiscations dried up the principal

* Jouffroy, *op. cit.*, p. 1302. There is a brilliant description of the passage from the political to the social revolution in Kautsky's *Communism in Central Europe*, p. 4.

† Nicolas, *op. cit.*, p. 201.

fund to which the poor had looked for charitable assistance.*

Modern socialism, as we said above, admits the omnipotence of the state in guiding and directing all the individual's economic and social activities; and the foundations of this idea of state omnipotence were laid by the reformers. When the legislative and governing power of the spiritual authority was abrogated by the Reformation, there remained no power to protect society from unbridled anarchy but the civil authority, which was elevated to a position of importance and unquestioned dictatorship that was never admitted in the Middle Ages.† Troeltsch sees in Luther's glorification of the secular authority the germ of mercantilism, and of the modern patriarchal idea of the state, which is not far removed from the socialist idea.‡ In some of the early Protestant sects, the subordination of the individual to the community was complete.§

We must remark in passing that the emancipation of the secular authority from the supervision of the spiritual was a two-edged weapon. It is true that it freed the civil authority from the control of the Church, but this simply meant that, if civil power were abused by those in power, there remained no legitimate and recognized method of deposing them. Absolute power is, in the very nature of things, impossible in this world; and one of the results of removing the constitutional checks on

---

* *Ibid.*, p. 197.   † Balmez, *op. cit.*, p. 252.
‡ *Soziallehren*, pp. 584, 589.
§ Möhler, *op. cit.*, vol. ii., p. 257. " As one of the principal causes of the Reformation was the strengthening of national self-consciousness, so conversely one of the most marked results of the movement was the exaltation of the State." (Preserved Smith, *The Age of the Reformation*, p. 593.)

the abuse of power is to render necessary the resort to revolutionary ones. The elimination of the spiritual power from politics at the Reformation freed the prince from the danger of deposition by the Church, but it opened the way to deposition by the people. It is therefore no exaggeration to say that the Reformation delivered the people to the despotism of the sovereign and the sovereign to the despotism of the people.*

But the change from the old to the new idea of the state had a further very important result. At the same time that there disappeared the supervision of the spiritual authority over the state there also disappeared the support which it gave it. All human authority in the Middle Ages rested on a spiritual foundation, and human superiority of every kind—political, social, and economic—was regarded as but a delegation of the Divine power of government. While this conception had the effect of investing offices of authority with responsibility and with duties, it had also the effect of placing them upon a sound foundation, and of greatly strengthening their powers of resistance to attack. The new conception robbed human authority of this responsibility and of these powers alike; and henceforward all superiority of man over man, whether in the political or the economic sphere, which could not be justified on purely rationalistic grounds, rested on force, and on force alone.†

The difficulty of justifying any sort of political or social inequality after the Reformation was increased by the doctrines of justification by faith alone and of predestination. The mediæval conception had pointed to man's life in this world and the next as a continued

* Nicolas, *op. cit.*, pp. 188-191.   † *Ibid.*, p. 139.

and unbroken existence, in the course of which rewards and punishments would be distributed in exact proportion to each man's merits; and the problem presented by the spectacle of the evil prospering and the good suffering was completely explained by this conception. The new doctrines of the reformers rendered this view of man's existence no longer tenable. The elect were saved and the rejected damned without any regard to their own merits or good works, and a fatalistic view of existence thus came to be developed. If the fate of each individual after death were irrevocably sealed by a Divine decree, what was there to hinder everybody from trying to make the present world as pleasant as possible, and what explanation could be given of the apparent injustices of social life, where some seemed to be blessed with plenty and affluence, and others condemned to penury and want ? In the old Catholic conception, each man was " the child of his own works "; and if his merits did not appear to be adequately rewarded in this world, there were two correctives at hand to repair this apparent injustice: charity, which softened the rigours of misfortune, and hope, based upon the knowledge of a future reward. This whole conception was overthrown by the doctrine of justification by faith alone.*

The new conception of social life led straight to communism. Once the doctrine of man's future state being in any way influenced by his own works was abolished, there was nothing to stand in the way of the most complete equalitarianism. Once it is admitted that the only reward of merit is in this world, it immediately follows that all existing irregularities of station,

* Nicolas, *op. cit.*, pp. 150-1, 384.

condition, and fortune, which do not rest on the merit of the possessor, are open to attack.   If the only purpose of society or wealth is to produce happiness in this world, and if it is true—and it can hardly be denied—that everybody has the right to be equally happy, there seems to be no answer to the claim for complete social and economic equality.   It is no answer to this claim to say that it involves revolution and the overthrow of existing society, because, according to its premises, existing society is profoundly unjust and unjustifiable, and ought to be overthrown as rapidly as possible.*

This new point of view involves a belief in the perfectibility of man's lot on earth by means of the perfecting of the institutions under which he lives. This is a characteristic belief of socialists of every school, who, however they may differ among themselves as to the form of institution that would produce the perfect society, are all agreed that some sort of institution would do so.   This belief involves the corollary that, if man's condition in existing society is not perfect, the way to make it so is by substituting some new form of society. It is the reform of the institution that is aimed at, in the belief that perfect institutions will create a society composed of happy individuals.   But, in order that this belief may be held, it is necessary to get rid of the old Catholic doctrine of original sin, which teaches that man is prone to evil by nature, and that no conceivable human institution can lead to perfection in this life, or can surmount man's naturally evil tendencies.   It is impossible for anybody to reconcile these two beliefs —the Catholic belief in original sin, and the socialist belief in the perfectibility of man through institutions.

* Nicolas, *op. cit.*, pp. 217-22, 419.

The unique service rendered to socialism by the Reformation was that it tampered with, and finally broke down the former, thus opening the way to the latter.

Luther's teaching on original sin tended towards extreme severity. According to him, original sin did not merely operate to incline man to evil, but it went so far as to suppress free will; man was only saved by the unchangeable, eternal, and inevitable will of God. Lutheran theologians held that, in fallen man, not the smallest good, however paltry, has survived; that corrupt nature, by itself, and of its own force, can do nothing but evil before God; that fallen man is all evil; and that all actual or personal sins are only the particular forms and manifestations of original sin—the boughs, as it were, and branches and blossoms of the wicked root and stem.* As is always the case, error in one direction led to a reaction in the other; and Zwingli taught that original sin was not a real sin at all, but merely an inclination to sin; that it did not in itself constitute a state of disgrace; and that one could only be reproved for the sins that were its consequences.† "From the one extreme opinion, that through Adam's fall all germs of good were utterly, even to the last vestige, eradicated from the whole human race, men passed to the other extreme, that even now man is in every respect as well-conditioned, and the universe wears as good an aspect for him as for the paradisiac man."‡ Möhler goes on to say: "As soon as the dam of vigorous but unenlightened feeling was broken through, nothing could prevent the whole doctrine of the fall being swept away."

* Nicolas, *op. cit.*, p. 229; Möhler, *op. cit.*, vol. i., p. 87.
† Nicolas, *op. cit.*, p. 230.   ‡ Möhler, *op. cit.*, vol. i., p. 91.

This actually happened. Calvin established, as a corollary from imputed justice, the doctrine that baptism could not be necessary to salvation; that it worked no forgiveness of sin nor infusion of grace in man, but was a seal only, and a token that we had received these favours.* The Socinians and the English Unitarians denied original sin altogether.†

The doctrine of original sin thus went through the usual course of contradiction, diminution, and final disappearance which is characteristic of doctrine in the hands of heretics; and the way was open for the proclamation of that great axiom which is at the base of all modern socialism, that man is born good. This axiom was unequivocally proclaimed by Rousseau, who was not slow to push it to its logical consequences. One of these consequences is that society is responsible for the depravity of man as we know him. Man is naturally good; but as we find him in society he is wicked; what can have debased him other than society ? The direct conclusion led to by this process of reasoning is that the remedy for the existing depravity of man is the destruction of society.‡

The steps by which the Reformation led to this characteristically socialist doctrine are admirably summarized by Nicolas: " Protestantism withdrew from the

* Bossuet, *Variations*, Book IX., Nos. 6 and 9.

† Möhler, *op. cit.*, vol. ii., pp. 320, 335; *Catholic Encyclopædia*, art. " Socinianism."

‡ Nicolas, *op. cit.*, p. 231; Baudrillart, *Études de la Philosophie morale*, vol. i., pp. 106-7. Morelly was the first to make use of Rousseau's teaching to advance the cause of communism. He argued that, as man was born good, he would be good once more if the institution of property were abolished, and that, if there were no property, there would be no avarice. (Rambaud, *op. cit.*, p. 629.)

tutelary authority of the Church Christian dogmas, notably the radical and universal dogma of original sin.

" The consequence is that natural reason, too weak to support the supernatural, destroys this doctrine by isolating it, and prepares the way for its fall by exaggerating it and minimizing it.

" The consequence is that this dogma disappeared soon from Protestantism itself.

" The consequence is, that when the Christian dogmas were overthrown, philosophism was able to substitute for them the dogmas of human thought, and lay down the principle that man is born good.

" The consequence is that it is society that depraves man.

" The consequence is that this depraving society must be remodelled from top to bottom, and that socialism, which undertakes to perform this mission, is admitted to execute its work."*

It is unnecessary further to labour the point that socialism postulates the perfectibility of man by means of the institutions under which he lives, and that this postulate is tenable only when the Catholic doctrine of original sin has been abandoned. Proudhon says: " It is a strange circumstance that it is the anathema fulminated by Rousseau against society that forms the basis of modern socialism. The theory of the innocence of man, correlative to that of the depravation of society, has prevailed. The immense majority of socialists, Saint-Simon, Owen, Fourier, and their disciples, the communists, the democrats, the progressives of

* P. 233. On the influence exercised on Rousseau by Protestantism, see Dide, *J. J. Rousseau, Le Protestantisme et la Révolution française*.

every kind, have solemnly repudiated the Christian myth of the fall, to substitute for it the system of an aberration of society."* Robert Owen, we are told by two modern socialistic writers, " founded his actions on the theory of the perfectibility of man by the amelioration of his surroundings."† We are not here concerned to point out the consequences to which this doctrine necessarily led; all we wish to do is to indicate that it is at the same time characteristically Protestant and characteristically socialist.

It is interesting to note in passing that the conception of man's perfectibility on earth is to be found in certain passages of the Old Testament. We saw in the last chapter that the preference of Protestants for the Old Testament was one of the causes which led to the excessive individualism of Protestantism; and it is a curious illustration of the truth, that a common point of departure is capable of leading to the most opposite errors, that the same insistence on the old dispensation led to certain socialistic notions. Kautsky points out that all the heretical communists and democrats based their order and institutions on the Old Testament;‡ and Laveleye has contended that modern socialism also has an Old Testament foundation. In the chapter on

---

* *Système des Contradictions économiques,* vol. i., p. 346.

† Morris and Bax, *op. cit.,* p. 209. Gide and Rist, in their *History of Economic Doctrines,* p. 238, say that Owen was the founder of social etiology, " the title given by sociologists to that part of their subject which treats of the subordination and adaptation of man to his environment." " Almost all socialists deny the fall of man, the inclination of the heart to evil, and the struggle of conscience against the passions, considered as a duty." (Migne, *Encycl. Théo.,* Sec. II., vol. xix., p. 1302; and see Bonar, *Philosophy and Political Economy,* p. 333.)

‡ *Communism in Central Europe,* pp. 250, 261.

Lassalle, in his book on *Contemporary Socialism,*
Laveleye says: " The Israelites have been almost everywhere the initiators or the propagators of socialism.
The reason is this: socialism is an energetic protest
against the actual order, based on iniquity, and an
ardent aspiration towards a better régime, where justice
would reign. But this is also the foundation of Judaism
in Job, in the Prophets, and in all the messianic aspiration. In the Israelite conception of the world, it is here
below that we must realize the greatest possible measure
of justice. From which it results that we must change
radically and by every means actual society."[*] Renan
drew attention to the same thing: " The Jew is not
resigned like the Christian. For the Christian, poverty
and humility are virtues; for the Jew, they are evils
from which one must defend oneself. The abuses and
violences, which leave the Christian calm, revolt the
Jew; and it is thus that the Israelite element has become,
in our time and in every country where it is present, a
great element of reform and of progress. Saint-Simonism
and the industrial and financial mysticism of our days
have half risen from Judaism."[†]   " The contemporary
socialist movement," says M. Batault, " must be considered, from the ideological point of view, as a kind of
messianic movement."[‡]

It is this messianic quality which most clearly distinguishes the social aims of socialism from those of the
Catholic Church in the Middle Ages. " The men of the
Middle Ages always kept before them the thought of a
world to come as the object of human endeavour. St.

* *Le Socialisme contemporain*, p. 419.
† Introduction to French translation of *Ecclesiastes*.
‡ *Op. cit.*, p. 167.

Augustine rejoiced to recognize that a City of God was rising on the ruins of the pagan world, and Aquinas delineated the lines on which it was framed; but neither of them would have thought of any earthly community as fulfilling their ideal of man. They looked on the Christian polity, with all its institutions, as the divinely instituted means of preparing man for the world to come; the mundane sphere was not regarded as a place for happiness, but for discipline. The conception of a utopia established on earth is not mediæval. As Troeltsch points out, it is humanistic, and dates from the Renaissance. The interpretation of the Kingdom of God as an earthly utopia differentiates modern Christian socialists from the writers on economics in the Middle Ages; the mediæval thinker never looked for a perfect mundane society, and many of them withdrew from the world; while socialists speak as if the chief duty of Christianity were to introduce happiness here and now."* The principal reason for this difference between the mediæval and socialist conception of the perfect society is the breaking down of the Catholic doctrine of original sin; and for this great change in the history of Christian thought the Reformation must take the responsibility.

The opposition between Catholicism and socialism arises from the fact that both attempt to cover the same field. Catholicism is not merely a religion, any more than socialism is merely an economic theory. As we have already seen, the acceptance of Catholic teaching on religious matters involves the acceptance of Catholic ethics in the domain of politics and economics, and a Catholic society is deeply coloured by the religious teaching of the Church. Socialism, on the other hand,

* Cunningham, *Christianity and Economic Science*, p. 6.

does not and cannot stop at the mere readjustment of men's economic relations in society; its basic principle, that man is in his present evil state because of evil institutions, cannot be restricted to questioning the institutions of inequality or of property, but inevitably advances to question every other institution as well— marriage, parental control, and religious institutions. Thus Catholicism and socialism both claim to regulate human life in all its aspects; and, as they are based on fundamentally opposite principles, it is inevitable that they must conflict, and that each must endeavour to destroy the other. " Starting from their belief in the supernatural," says Vandervelde, " religions—and particularly the Catholic religion—tend to regulate morals and, through morals, the entirety of social life. Starting from the transformation of the economic régime, socialism ends by revolutionizing the whole juridical, moral, philosophical, and religious superstructure. It is thus inevitable that the religions and socialism should come into contact with each other, although their points of departure are diametrically opposed."*

It is obvious also that the greater the territory covered by the dogmatic authority of the religion, the more severe will be its collision with socialism. It is possible that socialism might advance very far in a society consisting of persons of a purely subjective religion without coming into violent conflict with any religious belief antagonistic to itself; but it would be quite impossible for it to advance any distance in Catholic society without finding itself opposed on some vital point by the Church. That is why it is possible for socialist ideas to spread very rapidly among a com-

* " Le Socialisme et la Religion " in *Essais Socialistes*, p. 129.

munity of Christians who base their belief exclusively on their individual interpretation of scripture, and who trust for their salvation to an interior act of faith and trust in God—in other words, in a Protestant community. There is really nothing in the Bible which, on its face, appears to discountenance any of the characteristically socialist ideas; and that is why socialist propaganda finds evangelical Christians such an easy prey. Again, to quote Vandervelde: " In that which concerns evangelical Christianity, we do not see any obstacle to the acceptance by a disciple of Christ, relying solely-on his conscience, not accepting the authority of any Church, of any political or economic programme of any of the socialist parties. One can, without any contradiction, believe in the divinity of Christ and in the necessity of a social transformation in the sense of collectivism. As to the political or economic doctrines which are to be found in the Bible, they are manifestly too vague, too indeterminate, to offer any unanswerable opposition to other political or economic doctrines. . . . The very diversity and divergence of the interpretations which have been put upon the scriptures are sufficient to point to the conclusion, that, from the political and social point of view, one can find in the New Testament almost anything that one wants to find. Consequently, every man who does not submit to an interpretation imposed by authority can quite easily, taking his departure from the Gospels, end up in Tolstoyan anarchism or in democratic socialism. . . . No doctrinal or disciplinary authority attempts to prevent, or could prevent, Protestants from professing socialist opinions."*

* *Op. cit.*, pp. 134-9.

The actual opposition which exists between socialists and Protestants is founded on the remnants of the Catholic element which, as we have already shown, modern Protestantism still contains; but as this remnant is rapidly receding before the great destructive element of Protestantism, this opposition is becoming more and more feeble. Obviously, the advance of this destructive element, at the expense of the conservative element, not only tends to remove the inherent opposition between Protestantism and socialism, but also tends to weaken the weapons with which the former can withstand the latter. The more the principle of private judgment is admitted, the more hopeless it becomes to attempt to impose one's own opinions on other people. " If socialism," says Nicolas, " is the grown-up son of private judgment; if it is private judgment, passed from the religious order to the philosophical, political, and social order; if it is the growing insurrection against the Church, the state, and the home—evidently we can combat it only in its principle, private judgment, and by its contrary, authority. But the Protestant professes the principle of private judgment; how, then, can he invoke it ?"* Socialism, in a word, is social Protestantism; just as Protestantism was religious socialism.

* *Op. cit.*, p. 97.

CHAPTER I

Conclusion

THE thesis we have endeavoured to present in this essay is, that the two great dominating schools of modern economic thought have a common origin. The capitalist school, which, basing its position on the unfettered right of the individual to do what he will with his own, demands the restriction of government interference in economic and social affairs within the narrowest possible limits, and the socialist school, which, basing its position on the complete subordination of the individual to society, demands the socialization of all the means of production, if not of all wealth, face each other to-day as the only two solutions of the social question; they are bitterly hostile towards each other, and mutually intolerant; and each is at the same time weakened and provoked by the other. In one respect, and in one respect only, are they identical—they can both be shown to be the result of the Protestant Reformation.

We have seen the direct connection which exists between these modern schools of economic thought and their common ancestor. Capitalism found its roots in the intensely individualistic spirit of Protestantism, in the spread of anti-authoritative ideas from the realm of religion into the realm of political and social thought, and, above all, in the distinctive Calvinist doctrine of a successful and prosperous career being the outward and visible sign by which the regenerated might be known. Socialism, on the other hand, derived encouragement from the violations of established and prescriptive rights of which the Reformation afforded so many examples, from the growth of heretical sects tainted with communism, and from the overthrow of the orthodox doctrine on original sin, which opened the way to the idea of the perfectibility of man through institutions. But, apart from these direct influences, there were others, indirect, but equally important. Both these great schools of economic thought are characterized by exaggerations and excesses; the one lays too great stress on the importance of the individual, and the other on the importance of the community; they are both departures, in opposite directions, from the correct mean of the reconciliation of individual liberty with social solidarity. These excesses and exaggerations are the result of the free play of private judgment unguided by authority, and could not have occurred if Europe had continued to recognize an infallible central authority in ethical affairs.

The science of economics is the science of men's relations with one another in the domain of the acquiring and disposing of wealth, and is, therefore, like political science in another sphere, a branch of the science of ethics. In the Middle Ages, man's ethical conduct, like his religious conduct, was under the supervision and guidance of a single authority, which claimed at the same time the right to define and to enforce its teaching. The machinery for enforcing the observance of mediæval ethical teaching was of a singularly effective kind; pressure was brought to bear upon the conscience of the individual through the medium of compulsory periodical consultations with a trained moral adviser, who was empowered to enforce obedience to his advice by the most potent spiritual sanctions. In this way, the whole conduct of man in relation to his neighbours was placed under the immediate guidance of the universally received ethical preceptor, and a common standard of action was ensured throughout the Christian world in all the affairs of life. All economic transactions in particular were subject to the jealous scrutiny of the individual's spiritual director; and such matters as sales, loans, and so on, were considered reprehensible and punishable if not conducted in accordance with the Christian standards of commutative justice.

The whole of this elaborate system for the preservation of justice in the affairs of everyday life was shattered by the Reformation. The right of private judgment, which had first been asserted in matters of faith, rapidly spread into moral matters, and the attack on the dogmatic infallibility of the Church left Europe without an authority to which it could appeal on moral questions. The new Protestant churches were utterly unable to supply this want. The principle of private judgment on which they rested deprived them of any right to be listened to whenever they attempted to dictate moral precepts to their members, and henceforth the moral behaviour of the individual became a matter to be regulated by the promptings of his own conscience, or by such philosophical systems of ethics as he happened to approve. The secular state endeavoured to ensure that dishonesty amounting to actual theft or fraud should be kept in check, but this was a poor and ineffective substitute for the powerful weapon of the confessional. Authority having once broken down, it was but a single step from Protestantism to rationalism; and the way was opened to the development of all sorts of erroneous systems of morality. In the department of human affairs concerned with the economic activities of man, the old universally accepted code of justice fell into disregard, if not into ridicule; and its place was taken, on the one hand, by the theory that the only safe guide for man to follow in these affairs is his own personal interest, and, on the other hand, and partly as a reaction against this repulsive theory, that the individual has no right of initiative at all, but that his whole being must be subordinated to the welfare of the community. Both these theories would have been equally disapproved by the old, despised ethical authority of the Middle Ages, under whose régime they could not have flourished or developed; but, at the time when they arose, that old authority was no longer universally accepted, and there was no power in Europe strong enough to withstand the march of these two dangerous doctrines. The path to both capitalism and socialism had been opened by the Reformation.

The greatest damage caused by the Reformation was the disruption of the unity of Christendom. The evolution of a great society penetrated by Christian faith and embodying in its institutions the precepts of Christian morality ceased to be any longer possible when the dogmatic unity of Christendom was assailed and its central authority rejected. This explains why it was not alone the countries which adopted the Reformation that suffered from its evil effects; the blow directed against the authority of the Church wounded the Christian world as a whole, as well that part of it which remained faithful to the ancient teaching as that which embraced the new heresies. After the Reformation a great part of the energy which the Catholic Church had devoted in the Middle Ages to the development of philosophy and art, and to the propagation of the faith among pagans, had to be directed to protecting itself against the new enemies at its gate. It was precisely in the condition of a country suddenly convulsed by civil war; the efforts required to re-establish order and security within the realm, and to put down the disturbers of the peace, diverted the attention of the rulers from the pursuit of peaceful social reform, and weakened the power of the community against its external enemies.

The Reformation therefore left its mark on Catholicism as well as on Protestantism. The Catholic Church in the Middle Ages was engaged on a great assimilative process, in the course of which it absorbed into its philosophy all that was best in the pagan empires which it had displaced. The teachings of Aristotle and the lessons of Roman law had been gradually worked into the Christian scheme, and the Church was preparing to study and to assimilate the vast new wealth of ancient wisdom and culture which the Renaissance was displaying to the world, when all its attention was suddenly directed to combating a new danger which threatened the very foundation of its authority. Henceforth the Catholic Church was coerced by the necessities of the case to adopt a defensive attitude towards innovations of thought; in its fear of being accused of countenancing heretical opinions, it was frequently driven to display a caution which was liable to be confounded with obscurantism; and the fine energy which it had employed in the Middle Ages in the development of intellectual and social progress was diverted to the more exact definition of its doctrines and the enforcement of the discipline of its members. The Reformation was directly responsible for whatever there is of narrowness or reactionism in modern Catholicism.

The Reformation, therefore, coloured not only those who accepted it, but also those who rejected it. If it had not been for the deadly blow directed at its authority in the sixteenth century, the Catholic Church would have been able to change the whole colour of modern European civilization. If the ethical teaching of the scholastics had been allowed to develop freely and peacefully, there can be no doubt that it would have evolved side by side with the new developments of modern life, and would have proved perfectly adequate to meet all the necessities of the complex civilization of the present time; and, if the great charitable institutions of the Middle Ages had been suffered to pursue their course, it is equally certain that a great part of the terrible social problems of the industrial era would have been either mollified or avoided. Above all, the modern world, instead of being a battleground, studded with the hostile camps of capitalism and socialism and every other economic theory, would have been a harmonious society, in which all the members would be bound by identical ties of right and duty, and in which the conflicting claims of the individual and the community would be regulated by well-understood principles of justice, universally recognized and universally enforced. In other words, we would be living in an organic, and not in a critical, period.

The division of history into organic and critical periods we owe to Saint-Simon. During the organic periods mankind accepts with firm conviction some positive creed, while during the critical periods men lose their old convictions without attaining any new ones of a general authoritative character. The organic period of Christianity came to an end, and the critical period began, at the Reformation, when the authority of the Church was assailed, and the reign of private judgment inaugurated. This critical phase has lasted for 400 years, and it will continue until a new organic period can be begun by the universal acceptance of some common creed. The discovery of that creed is man's capital task to-day. Ever since the Reformation the old foundations of European life have been attacked by successive waves, first of Protestantism, and then of rationalism, until society has arrived at its present chaotic, formless, distracted condition. If the critical period continues much longer, European civilization will cease to be equal to the strain. In the economic world in particular, distraction reigns. Man is arrayed against man, and class against class, and nowhere is there to be found any sure guide or preceptor. The need is urgent for some social creed which will restore the harmony of human relationships, and will save Europe from tottering into the abyss which she seems to be rapidly approaching.

The quest after this creed has been the special mission of socialism, but the mission has failed. Socialists, usually with the best intentions, have not only failed to convince the adherents of the old order, but have failed to agree, even on first principles, among themselves. Even in the short course of its existence, socialism has disintegrated into a thousand different sects, each perfectly convinced of its own infallibility, and all mutually intolerant. This is merely another illustration of the obvious truth, that private judgment fails to produce the unanimity and certitude that are necessary to create a great world-governing principle; the disagreements among socialists are precisely similar to those among Protestants, and arise from the same cause. Authority must come from above, and cannot come from below.

We do not think that anybody seriously hopes at the present day that the reorganization of society can be achieved by socialism. The fatal tendency to disintegration among socialists themselves is sufficient to dispel any illusions that may have been harboured on this point. Besides, it must be remembered, as we pointed out above, that socialism is but a reaction against the excesses of individualism which found its most perfect expression in the works of the classical economists; and a movement which is merely a reaction in origin cannot hope to become a great constructive creed. If the abuses of capitalism were removed, the modern socialist movement would sink to a position of insignificant importance. The creed necessary to institute a new organic period of society will not be found in socialism any more than in capitalism; what is required is some system that will avoid the excesses of both these extremes. In Proudhon's words, we require to find the synthesis between the thesis of political economy and the antithesis of socialism.

It must be admitted that the hope of such a social creed emerging from the welter of present-day civilization is slight. The modern world is essentially anti-authoritative, and it is difficult to see how it can arrive at a social ethic that will command universal adherence.

The private judgment of individuals, unguided by any outside authority, may succeed in producing a philosophy, such as that formulated by the Stoics. But a philosophy can never supply the place of a religion, because it is in its very nature incapable of making a universal appeal. Indeed, it is hard to see how a philosophy could profoundly influence the life of a country governed on the democratic basis prevalent in Europe to-day. In any community where the governing power is in the hands of the people at large, the only alternative to an unprincipled régime and moral anarchy is the dominion of a generally recognized religious authority, competent to lead the people in ethical affairs. A philosophy can become an operative moulding force on the life of those states only which are governed by their wisest and best citizens; it can never profoundly affect the masses; and therefore cannot mould the policy of a state whose government is in the hands of the people at large.

The fact that the civil state is the only power authorized to prescribe and enforce the moral standards of social and economic life to-day presents a further obstacle to the growth of the new social ethical creed that is so urgently necessary, inasmuch as that creed, if it is to do the work required of it, must be cosmopolitan and common to all civilized nations. The social ethic of the Middle Ages was cosmopolitan, and took no notice of national frontiers; and the need for such an ethical system being cosmopolitan is a thousand times more urgent to-day than in the Middle Ages, because of the growth of international trading and the increased complexity of modern international relations. It is unnecessary to labour the point that it would be impossible

for any part of the modern world to attempt to re-
construct a new society animated by a higher social
ethic so long as its neighbours and competitors were free
to conduct their economic life on the old unregulated
lines.   Such an attempt could have but one result: the
pioneer of the new system would be economically
destroyed.   The need for this cosmopolitan co-operation
in the effort to ameliorate social conditions has been
recognized by the numerous conventions between states
on such subjects as sweated labour and the regulation
of working hours.   But such conventions, though highly
laudable, can touch but a fringe of the evils of modern
society.   When it comes to the introduction of a new
social ethic which will influence every transaction of
industrial and commercial life, no conventions can be of
any value, because it is the conscience, and not the
conduct, of the individual that must be affected.   So
long as the civilized world is divided into separate
nations—and the principle of nationality does not appear
to be weakening ; so long as the maxim of the political
infallibility of the majority is admitted; and so long as
the only power competent to enforce moral standards
in social life continues to be the state; so long will the
regeneration of the social life of the world by a new
ethical conception be impossible.

There is one institution and one institution alone
which is capable of supplying and enforcing the social
ethic that is needed to revivify the world.   It is an
institution at once intranational and international; an
institution that can claim to pronounce infallibly on
moral matters, and to enforce the observance of its
moral decrees by direct sanctions on the individual
conscience of man; an institution which, while respecting

and supporting the civil governments of nations, can claim to exist independently of them, and can insist that they shall not intrude upon the moral life or fetter the moral liberty of their citizens.   Europe possessed such an institution in the Middle Ages; its dethronement was the unique achievement of the Reformation; and the injury inflicted by that dethronement has never since been repaired.

INDEX